KEEP YOUR MOBILE PHONE AWAY OR DIGEST IT

Towards the end of man thinking by himself

ALPHONSE VANDERHEYDE

Translation by Christophe DZOU

Great Translator in Cameroon

(FR-ENG / ENG-FR)

(dzouchristophe94@gmail.com)

ISBN
Paperback 979-8-89519-856-8
Hardcase 979-8-89588-282-5

Translation by

Christophe DZOU - *Great Translator in Cameroon (ENG-FR / FR-ENG)*
(dzouchristophe94@gmail.com),
verified by the author.

By the same author

- **Nietzsche et la pensée bouddhiste**

- **Nietzsche et la pensée des brahmanes**, published by L'Harmattan, 2008, Paris.

- **Les acquis de la mort de l'homme (Volume 1: La philosophie de la mort de l'homme)**, published by
Connaissances et savoirs, 2017, Paris

- **La fin de l'éducation de l'homme (Volume 2: des Acquis de la mort de l'homme)**, published by Connaissances et Savoirs, 2020, Paris.

CONTENTS

Preamble for English-speaking readers   *vii*

Introduction: Mental Manipulation and Digital Intoxication   *ix*

PART ONE: KEEP YOUR MOBILE PHONE AWAY

Chapter 1

What does it mean to keep away your mobile phone?   2

Chapter 2

Smartphonic Nihilism: The Era of Emptiness, Speeches, and Images   6

Chapter 3

Scientists warn against the effects of screens - hyperconnectivity, the disease of the postmodern era.   25

Chapter 4

Is the smartphone ego hateful and dictatorial?   36

Chapter 5

Friends, or rather, Fake Smartphonic Friends   42

SECOND PART DIGEST YOUR MOBILE PHONE   46

Chapter 6

What Does It Mean to Digest Your Mobile Phone?   47

Chapter 7

The Mobile Phone and Artificial Life   50

Chapter 8

The Challenges of Digital Ethics   60

Chapter 9

Digital Culture, a Difficult Digestion   71

Chapter 10

The issue of our humanity - what are the human limits?   77

General Bibliography   *119*

PREAMBLE FOR ENGLISH-SPEAKING READERS

In 2023, I wrote this book in French and therefore in Western culture, which we know has been marked by Christianity for 20 centuries. But this Christian culture is no longer claimed in Europe: we are living in a kind of end of civilisation, the end of Christian culture. To understand this disaffection for the religious ideals of Christianity, we must always refer to Nietzsche›s formula: «God is dead», meaning that Europeans no longer believe in God and therefore their values are discordant. They think on their own, without God and without ecclesial Christianity. This loneliness is forging another culture: the culture of the death of God and the death of man.

This new culture raises the issue of the mobile phone, its use, and the excessive exposure to smartphone screens. To be, or not to be on our mobile is the fundamental question of our digital world. It›s a global problem affecting every culture and civilisation, especially young people at school or university. Is there a desire to corrupt minds, to prevent them from thinking by themselves? Are we witnessing mental manipulation by the giants of the net: GAFAM?

It should also be noted that our smartphone world is leading us towards a modification of the human being through the fanciful adventures of transhumanism and posthumanism. Is a world of people who are half human and half robot desirable? Are we heading for a world controlled by the state? Never in the history of people and cultures have humans sought to modify themselves through techno-sciences. Is digital technology the end of human culture?

English-speaking readers, particularly from India, Africa, and Latin America, can understand my comments in the light of the declining culture in Europe. Behind this cultural decline, are we to see a refusal to be human, in other words, a move away from wisdom? Do we need to work on becoming human again, as Joseph Dhanaswamy suggests[1]? Because, deep down, man's desire has created a world without relationships, without pity, without charity, without humility[1].

---

[1] Joseph Dhanaswamy, "Becoming Human", BlueRose Publishers, New Delhi, London, 2021

INTRODUCTION
MENTAL MANIPULATION AND DIGITAL INTOXICATION

According to Nietzsche, for a long time, the earth has been a madhouse. These words still resonate in our drifting postmodernity, in our end of civilisation, in the agony of the materialistic and neopagan man. Why so much madness and excess in technology, especially in its use as if our already disordered world needed more confusion, ineptitude, and laziness of reason? The technological advances that are praised weigh heavily on our materialistic civilisation. For example, are screens a negative acquisition of our period of the death of man and the supposed death of God? On this point, I had written in the first two volumes of the "Acquisitions of the Death of Man" that for more than two centuries, postmoderns have been living poorly on the ruins of the death of God and man. However, this supposed double death does not necessarily herald the decline and end of ecclesial Christianity. Indeed, we are not at the end of Western, European Christian civilisation, but at the agonising end of neopaganism. For two centuries, we have become neopagans in rebellion against God and against man. But the postmoderns seem to remain Christians by their morality: they practice a "Christianity without Christ" (Nietzsche's expression). Today, postmodern civilisation has divorced itself from the sacred, mystery, transcendence. Everything is allowed, everything is crumbling. Yet, irresistible tensions remain after the shattering of Western culture: once, all spheres of religion, morality, politics, and education were held by ecclesial Christianity. With the death of God and man, these spheres are free, but they are in crisis.

In this context of the end of civilisation, postmodern technology is not immune to this crisis. We write this book to show the harmful effects of man's hyperconnectivity with his smartphone. This hyperconnectivity is unfolding peacefully before our eyes, so are we witnessing the end of man who thinks for himself? The postmodern is contaminated by his multiple connections. In this, he is a man ignorant of the harmful effects of his activities on screens. We do not want the end of the connected man, because we must deal with the digital, but we suggest the end of the man who is too connected, that is, he knows how to digest his connections and leave room to think by his own strength.

Certainly, for more than two centuries, we have been in the end of a neopagan civilisation. So, in this context, does the mobile phone also precipitate us into this end of civilisation? Is there a double end of civilisation? But also, what about our human way of thinking? Should we accept, without question, the need to be dominated by the phone, hyperconnectivity?

Behind the illegitimate hyperconnectivity, do we believe that we have genuine relationships with others? Indeed, what do we do with others in flesh and blood behind the screens? The digital age has caused a significant additional upheaval in our already sick postmodernity. Is it possible to save the man who thinks for himself, who knows how to digest and control his phone? Beware of digital manipulation and intoxication through the almost solemn contemplation of smartphone screens.[2]

---

[2] Alphonse Vanderheyde: «La philosophie de la mort de l'homme» (2017), «La fin de l'éducation de l'homme» (2020), Two volumes published by Connaissances et Savoirs, Paris.

PART ONE

KEEP YOUR
MOBILE PHONE AWAY

CHAPTER 1

WHAT DOES IT MEAN TO KEEP AWAY YOUR MOBILE PHONE?

Here, it is hardly a question of waging war on screens or mobile phones. It would be absurd to want to eliminate the laptop, but we have the right to alarm, to analyse, to ask to put away the screens, to stop working digitally on the screens. If we use screens for professional work, who can criticise this attitude? But when the laptop is not a professional or school work tool, we have the legitimate right to question its use, its many exponential connections, which are often pitiful. That's why, let's not waste time, put away our cell phone, and use it wisely.

This storage needs to be clarified in relation to the lessons learned from the death of man. In our context of the end of civilisation, it seems impossible to escape the temptation of screens. The young and the not so young, passive in front of screens, have never taken seriously the manipulation of their conscience because they are cyber-dependent. They hardly realise the smartphone disaster. There is a kind of "youth digital radicalisation" here. The young are particularly in this digital prison. For example, on the screens of their mobile phones, they display their biography on a planetary level. Are they aware of their fall into nihilism, into the void of values, into this end of man thinking for himself? Precisely, the man connected to infinity takes on the meaning of an end to our humanity. Here is a chasm in which postmodernists remain without real reflection. Let us therefore enter into disconnection, into "dedigitalisation." Let us sometimes put away our screens for a real life with others.

Far from being an invitation to destroy the digital phone, our present work aims to examine the reasons for organising, setting aside, and mastering our mobile phone. It will not necessarily be a matter of examining one reason at a time, but of becoming aware that these new technologies, often misused, are like thorns in our hands. How have screens led us into this digital dependence? Let's free ourselves from the mobile phone. Let's undergo a digital detox.

We do not call for breaking the cell phone, but for putting it away in front of others: when talking to someone, nothing is more impolite than browsing on your smartphone. One can hardly do both at the same time. Let's choose to put it away in our pocket to give our full attention to others. Smartphone users are not above the laws of decency, good manners, and politeness.

To put away one's phone is to say no to collective force-feeding. We are not geese, and yet we are subjected to an information overload. Nietzsche, in his time, wrote about historical fever in his "Unfashionable Observations": history is detrimental to life in that we learn what has already been. According to Nietzsche, youth undergo force-feeding of historical knowledge: they only learn and therefore they are sick. Postmodern individuals are also sick from screens. They do not learn; they only contemplate, they move from one connection to another without taking the time for discernment. Is it really necessary to live in a constant connectivity? Hyperconnectivity is one of the evils of our decadent century. The invention of "unlimited data plans" has introduced the young and the old into a chaos of connections. It seems that we are in a hyper-connected jungle where the only rule is to harm the weak-minded, the ignorant, the learners, the young, and the old.[3]

What a waste of time spent searching on one's smartphone for hours! Often, digital time is not intellectual time, nor a time for reflection, nor a time for real general culture. The best time is the one found outside of our phone: that time elevates our mind.[4]

---

[3] Stéphane Blocquaux: Le biberon numérique, Artège, 2021, Paris.

[4] Catherine Price: Lâche ton téléphone. Programme de détox digitale, édition Librairie générale française, 2018.Paris.

Our general culture. While the fleeting glances we cast at the smartphone constantly disrupt our lives. Because we are led by this illegitimate necessity to forcibly check our messages... So, let's put away our screens and turn our gaze towards others. For example, let's directly talk to our friends. Let's act in a present manner immediately. Discussion, just discussion, all public discussion. Talking with others, spending time with them, is another way to distance ourselves from our phones and humanise our postmodernity a little. The competition introduced between smartphone connections and our friends shows an abyss, something incompatible: humanising the phone is a deception since our screens are less human than humans. We feel like we are in an era of emptiness, of nonsense. Because ultimately, it is man that we objectify and the phone becomes more human in appearance. But what loneliness in all smartphone connections. Let's acknowledge that we are mistaken about humanity. Let's put away our phones to become human again, to escape from this life of multiplied connections, while being disconnected from true life. The essential thing is to regain our lost humanity from the smartphone invasion. But it is always difficult, nowadays, to break free from our digital prison.

We know with Socrates that discussion is what resolves issues in the community. But with the advent of the smartphone, discussion is silent, visual, fast, and confusing. Written discussion, through screens, takes on a wild form: the smartphone is characterised by wild, anarchic, jerky, and shapeless discussion. In reality, it is wild writing: a digital dictatorship. How can one spend so much time with insipid, inconsistent, silent messages, emails? The deafening silence of these exchanges is a sensation that no longer shocks smartphone enthusiasts. Reading messages is hardly like reading a paper letter. Because reading a letter received by mail allows for a thoughtful response. Precisely, this time for reflection no longer exists in the fleeting readings on the screen. With the smartphone, one is always in haste and thoughtlessness. That is why it is good to put away one's phone during the week, to stop being constantly connected, to open one's smartphone at a specific time for thirty minutes a day. Let's flee from these digital and therefore artificial relationships.

Furthermore, the overactivity on the smartphone makes us believe that we are important, that we are the centre of the world. Because we display ourselves in front of the whole world, this smartphone narcissism completely disqualifies inner life. With disproportionate connections, the young or older user of screens forgets that inner life is more important than external life with its noise. Inner life can be called a certain way of detaching oneself for a while from the tumult of the external world. In our postmodernity, we no longer take the time for meditation, withdrawal, stopping all external activity to focus on the essential: reflection, just reflection, all reflection. Even before the smartphone, the postmodern was a prisoner of television, radio, and constant background noise. Today, this background noise and the images viewed are an infinite amplification. Let's not fall into this drug of multiplied connections (this visual dependence makes us sick unknowingly).[5]

---

[5] We know that Heraclitus of Ephesus had enough of the noise of the Ephesians, of the crowd of the many always incapable of thinking, of reflecting. Cf. Heraclitus, Fragments (translated by Marcel Conche), P.U.F., 1987, Paris.

CHAPTER 2

SMARTPHONIC NIHILISM: THE ERA OF EMPTINESS, SPEECHES, AND IMAGES

1. DEFINITION OF SMARTPHONIC NIHILISM: THE THOUGHT OF EMPTINESS WITHOUT CONCEPT

We have already studied the concept of nihilism in our two previous researches of "Acquired by the Death of Man".[5] Let us remember that we have been in a nihilistic period for 200 years. The ideals of Christianity, belief in God, have fallen (seemingly). For Nietzsche, nihilism has the meaning of "nothing has meaning,"[6] supreme values become devalued[7], because they come from a deepening feeling of nothing.[8] This nihilism is the consequence of the supposed death of God, that is to say of the Christian religion and consequently of Christian culture. The two are linked. By killing God, man has killed the Christian culture to which he belongs by definition, because it was shaped by her for 18 centuries. God is dead means for Nietzsche that the values forged by ecclesial Christianity are depreciating. However, our European culture is a Christian culture or forged by the ideals of Christianity. By removing the ideals of Christianity, what remains is nihilism, the emptiness of values. Likewise, killing God amounts to killing man because God and man are linked. This brutal double death explains the nonsense and lack of hope of postmodernists. From then on, our postmodernity finds itself in a cultural impasse, in multiplied crises: crisis of education, of the economy, of morality, of politeness. We are at the end of civilisation, clearly visible in the experience of postmodernists. This

6

nihilism takes the form of chaos, in the actions of our contemporaries, in the impasse of values.

It is in this Nietzschean nihilism that smartphonic nihilism is established. The irruption of screens (smartphone, internet, SMS, Facebook, Instagram, Discord, Twitter, etc.) has caused our postmodernity to sink into the chaos of ideas, into the anarchy of thought. This is smartphone nihilism. Indeed, through the invasion of permanent connections to social networks, a life emptied of man and God is taking shape. This reminds us of the idea of the death of God in Nietzsche's philosophy. The smartphone appeared in our already nihilistic period. Only the screens freeze us even more and almost definitively in nihilism, in the end of civilisation. This smartphone nihilism is another form of illness of connected postmoderns, slaves of the digital cell phone through addiction to social networks and their consequences, such as the absence of critical thinking, of reasoning, of reflection, of living together. To this deep void, we can give the name of smartphone nihilism.

Indeed, this void is perceptible: nihilism is made up of contradictory, often unconscious behaviours in front of screens, such as constantly looking at your smartphone. What do we learn from its multiplied connections? We should retain the feeling of emptiness and weariness in front of a plethora of images, in front of the same groups, in front of publications, and incentives to look without even being hungry. Nihilism here takes the form of routine, decline, idleness, and solitude. The force-feeding of texts and images translates into active nihilism. The smartphone fan is overtrained to blissful contemplation of screens.

Smartphone nihilism is indeed in the void of concepts because we are running empty in connections and reconnections. What remains of screen contemplations? There remains an overflow transformed into empty because nothing is fixed. We borrow from nihilism the expression of the concept of emptiness without concept: the smartphone fan believes that we find information, photos, texts useful for his life; in reality, the whole thing is a deception. Is there something serious behind our digital activities? It's not just the smartphone illusion, that is to say, the thought of emptiness without concept, since we are dominated by the need to constantly look at the phone. And so, there is no longer any real space to think.[6789]

2. THE SMARTPHONE NIHILISM, THE ABSENCE OF DEBATE OF IDEAS.

Smartphone nihilism is found in the absence of debate of ideas: the meaning of the discussion disappears under the permanent contemplation of screens. By constantly reading messages and information on your smartphone, you have the impression of participating in the debate of ideas and defending your convictions. In reality, by showing off, by displaying your photos, your words, you are outside of the Socratic style public discussion. We hardly try to open up to discussion. We know that Socrates made dialogue his philosophical principle. In our digital world, reason, that is to say the confrontation of ideas to know who is telling the truth, is no longer used in the manner of the pre-Socratics, nor of Socrates. Reasonable dialogue is no longer the criterion for debate because there are no longer any real discussions between smartphone users since images and texts jostle and circulate in all directions on the screens. Often, smartphone discussions are meaningless, anarchic, truncated, and consequently they contain no serious analysis, no invitation to meditation, to reflection, a question never asked. This method of hypercoverage of information blocks time for reflection: we occupy, we cover the smartphone with empty speech. This annihilation of reason, of the falling asleep of reason, takes the form of a smartphonic nihilism, that is to say an impossibility of thinking for oneself and of thinking with others. We would not be very far from unreason in the relationship with the smartphone, a sort of smartphone nonsense...

---

[6] Alphonse Vandervelde: La philosophie de la mort de l'homme, Volume 1, Les acquis de la mort de l'homme, published by Connaissances et Savoirs editions, 2017. P20, Paris Alphonse Vandervelde: La fin de l'éducation de l'homme. Volume 2: Acquis de la mort de l'homme, published by Connaissances et Savoirs editions, 2020, Paris.

[7] Nietzsche: Fragments Posthumes, volume III, XII, autumn 1885, 2[127], p. 179, collection colli montinari Paris

[8] Nietzsche: Fragments Posthumes, volume XIII, 9 [35], p. 278, Paris.

[9] Nietzsche: Fragments Posthumes, Volume XII, 11 [228], p. 278, Paris.

Our attention is great in front of screens, and therefore, this fascination with images and writings opposes any questioning. From then on, this thought of the void, its concept is contrary to philosophy, in particular to Greek philosophy: smartphone life no longer questions our values, our information, our text messages; we no longer take care of real dialogue, of thinking for yourself and with others (our relationships are reduced to formless contacts); false dialogue through social networks leads us to the chaos of our postmodernity. Because these "dialogues" are always motivated by the constraint of the immediate: occupying the screens, emptiness is not permitted. However, the pseudo-dialogues exchanged on social networks never get to the bottom of things; we no longer know how to take the time to mature our thoughts. This is also smartphone nihilism.

Postmodernism is dominated by news and fake news. He ignores it because his thoughts are numbed. How often he is driven by the visible effects of the smartphone and by the need for social networks to direct his psyche towards this or that information. We listen blissfully, we look at the screens while losing our own thoughts: this way of misguiding reason is one of the great harmful effects of our a-Christian, anti-Christian postmodernity. It is impossible to think freely through connections and reconnections: a life excessively connected to the smartphone is a life emptied of the exercise of intelligence. We no longer think; we no longer dialogue with ourselves.

This shows that social media is nihilistic and even teaches the active nihilist. Indeed, our time has a horror of real debate. Postmodernism has forced itself into a ready-to-think state, into a mould of indigestible images, of fragmented cultures, of the dictatorship of exponential images and pure emotion. Smartphone nihilism is the absence of analysis and discernment in the permanent connection with social networks. For example, we wonder what the use of displaying ourselves is, of showing ourselves, of putting up photos of ourselves. It is there, a dictatorship of oneself, of one's self invading the formless screens. In reality, we distort information about ourselves, but also about the others.

This smartphone nihilism is also found in fake news and ordinary news. Information is systematically presented in the form of "woke" without our knowledge. The "woke" movement is one of the religions of the postmoderns. It no longer consists of debating ideas in the manner of

Greek philosophy but in a way of disqualifying any other form of thought. The "wokes" have been inspired by philosophers such as Derrida, Foucault, Beauvoir, Sartre. For them, everything is constructed, everything we consider obvious, natural like gender relations (...) is the product of social and cultural construction that is arbitrary. The goal is to deconstruct established culture. For example, Sartre's formula "existence precedes essence" means that man exists, he defines himself afterwards: it is I who decide my life, to do what I want. Religion, tradition, society should no longer intervene: they no longer decide my culture, they hardly participate in the construction of my life, freedom is absolute. Building one's essence is one thing, but forgetting that one is part of a culture, a way of life, is another way of building oneself alone, of thinking only of oneself, of relegating human history to oblivion. So, we fall into cultural and intellectual anarchy.

This thought out of culture in nihilism is called the politically correct by American academics. We regret the drift of woke thinking (from the English "awake") because it rejects debate and floods social networks with meaningless news that never give us anything to think about or analyse. Woke thinking seems to be the major thought of social networks. In reality, we are forbidden to think differently by these wokes. A right to refuse offence is established. We must think like everyone else. Beyond the for or against, where is the public debate, intellectual confrontation, and consultation of opposing ideas and theses? This neutralisation of public debate refers to smartphone nihilism or information nihilism, meaning that our ideas, our way of thinking are shaped by the dictatorship of news and therefore social networks. We are no longer allowed to think in terms of Greek philosophy. We must think in terms of the sub-philosophy of wokism and ambient journalism.

The word "woke" is a concept that is part of the American cultural network. Let's understand the meaning of the word "woke": "It is either the past participle of the verb to wake, or the shortcut for being awake. It means, in a way, to be alert to current problems [...]; it is now used to denounce discrimination in all its forms... It is also mocked as a state of permanent indignation that strikes blindly in all directions."

Wokism is present in all spheres of American society. For example, McCarthyism can be compared to wokism in that it denounced internal enemies. There is indeed a kind of witch hunt against any deviant behaviour. Wokism takes the form of "Cancel culture"; it is about ostracising and excommunicating all those who think differently. Social networks are the instruments of "cancel culture" decided by a minority: certain positions that go against woke thinking are censored. It is surprising that minority discourses want to become the majority and, above all, they demand the blocking of discussion. All spheres of society (politics, education, rewriting of history, press...) are put to the test of woke. Thus, wokism has become a set of demands establishing an end to discussion on gender theory, identity... This doctrine creates a kind of culture war, a political escalation.

In sum, faced with the single thought, the smartphone world is reduced to wokism.[10][11][12]

Dangerous because, according to Rod Dreher, it is a soft totalitarianism. Here, the word totalitarianism does not refer to a state practicing dictatorship; it is a totalitarianism that disguises itself with a soft, gentle face and therefore advances masked. With our smartphone life, we are not in the Gulag, but it resembles it due to the obligation of "politically correct", of an illegitimate wokism. According to Rod Dreher, wokism engages in a radical exploitation of the decadent preferences of the postmodern man. Those who do not share this woke party line are destroyed (their businesses, their reputation, their careers). They are then accused of all evils. For example, if a postmodern rejects gender theory, they are excluded from institutions. Therefore, it is a totalitarianism that does not reveal its name. René Gérard already showed concern for victimisation; this is indeed fanaticism, a permanent neo-inquisition. For example, digital giants (Facebook, Amazon...) collect our personal data to guide us in our lives, in our rights. They seek to impose their standards on us and divert us from true discussion.

Wokism is the double product of the death of man and the death of God. One must think like everyone else. The smartphone has accentuated a certain nihilistic way of thinking about life: all values are equivalent. One no longer has the right to propose their own values, as they are in discord

---

[10]   Eugénie Bastié: La guerre des idées, édition Robert Laffont, 2021, Paris.

[11]   Anne Toulouse: Wokisme, éditions du Rocher, 2022, p.12

[12]   Article by Philippe Forest: «La querelle du woke» in Etudes, September 2023, p. 43-54, Paris

with the single thought. In the hands of manipulators, wokism is a weapon against true dialogue. It dangerously sets the norms according to which we are authorised to think; we are guided in our choices. Therefore, we no longer have the right to think outside the framework set by wokism. We are indeed in a smartphone dictatorship, a dictatorship of wokist thought. Smartphone users are unaware of the ravages of wokist dictatorship. This is yet another reason to put away your phone or to be attentive to the crushing of our own thoughts, our own free way of thinking without intermediaries.

The "wokist" doctrine is the result of our neo-pagan and therefore anti-Christian life. It is a dictatorship of thought: we are forced to adhere to this wokist vision of our postmodernity. We are truly in a nihilistic period because it demands thinking against tradition, and therefore we no longer have a tradition, or more precisely, wokism wants to establish a new tradition. So, what should we do with our culture stemming from Christianity? The tragedy of the postmodern, through its genuflections before digital screens, is that it rejects its Christian cultural roots. It believes that the world begins with it. It then establishes a new way of thinking, a thought of emptiness, and especially one that does not call for any public discussion. Are we still in Socratic philosophy?

3. IS FREEDOM OF EXPRESSION THREATENED BY THE GAFAM?

Our non-Christian postmodernity continues to degrade through the digital coup, as it is the tech giants (Google, Amazon, Facebook, Apple, Microsoft) who govern the internet and thus shape our thinking. Now, might makes right. We have simply returned to a state of nature, governed by the law of the jungle, but it is an invisible jungle that thrives on ignorance and addiction to the digital. There is indeed a direct threat to democracy here. The use of social networks can lead to disasters in the form of a major crisis of democracy as in America: on January 6, 2020, the call to storm the Capitol in Washington. Besides the democratic irresponsibility, note that the rioters obey their impulses and not their reason. Here, with a simple tweet, one can call for violence, for uprising to express disagreement with the election results, so that the democratic game is no longer respected.

We have been living in a digital putsch for 25 years. There was a time when social networks were believed to be tools for liberating speech, for consolidating democracy, and a counter power among others.[13]

In reality, we do not realise enough the manipulation of consciences. Digital companies engage in permanent operations of stealing private data, directing our desires, and controlling our freedoms. Digital capitalism takes our personal data, interprets it, and then considers it as its own private property, all with the complicity of the States in postmodern democracies. The power of the digital escapes the citizens: they are subjected to the dictatorships of the GAFAM, that is, private groups that have never been elected to control thought and guide our postmodern civilisation.

The rise of algorithms and the spread of false information are major plagues of our time. We can compare the tyrannical power of the GAFAM to that of the leaders of the industrial revolution who had all the rights. In the era of the digital revolution, democrats have abandoned control of the digital to companies. We are witnessing, before and after the pandemic, the dictatorship of anti-social networks. Social media users avoid becoming aware of this dictatorship of information, orientation, and dissemination of news. Internet users in democracies are under surveillance. For example, in 2013, the director of the CIA asked internet companies to "collect and retain everything without time limit." The big internet companies are starting to control public debate. These are no longer debates but unhealthy orientations of thought: postmodern companies want to control how we think, speak, consume, and entertain ourselves. Obviously, they do not encourage buying books by Plato, Kant, or Bergson… All these falsely ancient philosophical thoughts are still relevant. But by a magic trick of sinister internet companies, we find ourselves embarked on a certain way of thinking, believing, and living. The supremacy of technology is exerted without our knowledge. Who will denounce this? The philosopher always has his usefulness. For example, Socrates always denounced the violent speeches of the sophists Gorgias, Polos, Thrasymachus. He was able to show the absurdity of their fanciful theses like scratching when you have scabies and even adds Gorgias if it pleases us, we can scratch our whole life. So, such a thesis is ridiculed by

---

[13]   Rod Dreher: Résister au mensonge. Vivre chrétiens dissidents, édition Artège, 2021. Paris.

Socrates. The sophist Gorgias is in no way aware of the shortcomings of his position. Similarly, today, the giants of digital technology make fun of us and we react little because we have been contaminated for 25 years by the spread of news and fake news. How did we come to read and reread fake news? We want information and we find social networks, now anti-social networks. The GAFAM only seek financial gain. We are no longer in a social construction of reality but in a social deconstruction of our postmodernity in multiplied crises.

Let us be aware of the Machiavellian world drawn by social networks. Let us not become impeccable consumers. Our postmodernity is caught in the illegal and immoral monopoly of internet giants. No one has filed a complaint against Facebook for ending competition by acquiring WhatsApp and Instagram. Economic logic has taken precedence over digital ethics.

There are already 2.5 billion Facebook users, but do we pay attention to freedom of expression? Never in our postmodernity have men been so deceived and so little free to control information on social networks. We no longer know what freedom of expression and public debate are because we are too subjected, without our knowledge, to the dictatorship of digital giants. These seek only financial gain in billions of dollars. This is an activity contrary to philosophy and common sense.[14][15][16][17][18]

This deficit in freedom of thought perfectly matches the natural data of our postmodernity, insofar as the GAFAM appear at a time of the end of civilisation, crisis of the established religion, crisis of education (crisis of the classical transmission of knowledge and the exercise of reason...). We were already anaesthetised by the disappearance of 20 centuries of Christian culture, or more precisely, our world was already troubled by the rejection of Christian culture. But the void is filled (so we believe)

---

[14]   Alexis de Tocqueville: De la démocratie en Amérique, Garnier-Flammarion, 2010, Paris.

[15]   Shoshana Zuboff: l'age du capitalisme de surveillance, édition Zulma, 2020, Paris

[16]   Le coup d'état numérique, in Courrier International, Hors-série avril-mai 2021, Paris

[17]   Comité national pilote d'éthique du numérique. Pour une éthique du numérique, P.U.F., 2021, Paris.

[18]   Le coup d'État numérique, ibid., p.16-17, Paris.

by artificial intelligence. We had lost the fundamental data of the culture stemming from Christianity, and now on the ruins of our end of civilisation is grafted the "cancel culture", the woke culture, another way of thinking that is undemocratic and unchristian. To the multiplied crises, we add a crisis of contemporary democracy, in the form of an attack on true public debate.

Social networks have reshaped public debate by forcing all internet users to think the same way. Digital technology, in the form of anti-social networks, standardises discourse by avoiding public debate. In the era of exchanges, paradoxically, there is no longer any debate. The Socratic style of debate has given way to attacks without the right of reply. Information is disseminated without an invitation to public debate, or more precisely, the debate has shifted in meaning: it consists of formless SMS messages, tweets. The debate is no longer quite the meeting of an "I" and a "you", but the artificial meeting of virtual friends, dry information often presented in a truncated manner.

Paradoxically, public debate struggles to exist in anti-social networks. This absence is strongly linked to our postmodern, non-Christian, and always critical era. Everyone believes they are thinking for themselves, but they are influenced or simply reproduce what they have heard, what they have read on social networks. Postmodernity no longer relies entirely on values stemming from Christianity, but on values of constant free criticism, disorder of thought, and a lack of confrontation of projects. Debate has lost its utility: there is too much talk and nothing interesting is said. The postmodern speaks anarchically on their smartphone because they embody anarchic, dissolved values. They believe they are creating new values by staging societal laws and limitations in bioethics, but in reality, they no longer know how to debate and defend their ideas. This is indeed a nihilism of ideas, or more precisely, everyone must think the same thing on different major subjects. Postmodernity vehemently rejects those who think and live differently. Their lifestyle choices disturb because they still think of life in Christian terms. Thus, today, we are guided by neo-pagan values coming directly from the internet: inner life is targeted. It is the overflowing and entirely external life that the GAFAMs exalt because they need to occupy the media space and direct our thinking. For example, Facebook positions itself as an arbiter of truth. However, we know that truth is a subject of discussion.

It is found in and through reasonable dialogue. If it is given from the outside as by the GAFAMs, public debate dies. Therefore, it is better to put away one's phone than to be guided by internet companies.

Internet users have the impression of talking a lot through emails and social networks, but what do they really say? Nothing very reasonable and useful, it seems. And even, we believe we are in the era of digital communication and therefore we believe we are constantly talking and having debates, but in reality, we are talking banally. We are witnessing the symptoms of a civilisation's end. Indeed, our postmodernity is anarchic in its intertwined and therefore unintelligible ideas. We do not speak; we exchange few true words on social networks. On the contrary, we are trapped in a terrible, deafening silence because we are alone. Consequently, with the GAFAMs, our postmodernity sinks further into the end of man, that is, into the end of man thinking for himself because of the smartphone support. It is not the smartphone that should think for me,[19][20]

It is I who must make the effort to think. It is not me who needs the smartphone; it is the smartphone that must adjust to my decisions, my ideas, my will to address problems in a reasonable speech. However, with the exaltation of smartphone life (as if we were born with a smartphone, or we were already connected), the postmodern has lost its freedom to think, to express itself, because it has unwittingly become a slave to the mobile phone, a slave constantly spied on by the GAFAMs. Today, we are faced with propaganda on the internet. This propaganda is no longer reserved for totalitarian regimes but also for democracies. It is an attempt to influence people (David Colon: "Propaganda. Mass Manipulation in the Contemporary World," Belin, 2019, p.13). Through the falsification of truth in the digital industry, the aim is to colonise minds, especially those of the young, and prevent them from thinking for themselves: thinking through the smartphone is an exercise for screen contemplators.

---

[19] Jacques Attali: Histoires des médias, Fayard, 2021, p. 39, Paris.

[20] Digital technology and its use through smartphones appear as a coup d'état in thinking, taking the form of a smartphone dictatorship, a totalitarianism.

4. CULTURAL NIHILISM

One of the sources of knowledge today comes from smartphones and television (BFM TV, Cnews, LCI, etc.), but what a subculture! In reality, it is multiplied information, repetitive, and directing a certain way of thinking in a vacuum. Where is general culture? Information on the news and passionate and automatic consultations of mobile screens have never constituted an authentic culture. Where is the true knowledge that encourages us to reflect, to think for ourselves? Continuous information is more theatrical than thoughtful and, therefore, it is a kind of disposable press, disposable information because it has no perspective. Immediate commentary often takes the form of confusing information. What certainty in the comments made by specialists or not! They seem like information gurus who impose on us the way we receive and understand the news. And, therefore, we would do better to put away our screens and open them once a day, for example from 7:30 p.m. to 8 p.m.

We then live in an era of smartphone nihilism, which here takes the form of cultural nihilism. We are in the void of culture when the internet provides infinite cultural data that is often difficult to exploit. We call the misuse of the smartphone cultural nihilism, that is to say, screens do not increase our culture; on the contrary, they "de-culture" us. What a waste of time! Reading digital screens is opposed to diligent reading of a book (novel, philosophy), and digitised books have hardly promoted reading or sales. It follows that the time spent on screens is never useful time, cultural time but nihilistic time, a bit of zero time. Never has general culture been so free and within our reach, but we have never lost spelling, grammar, general culture so much. We become uneducated by frequenting too many formless and indigestible screens. Cultural nihilism has appeared at the heart of our postmodernity because we are too immersed in hyperconnectivity in opposition to authentic general culture. The more we are connected, the less we cultivate ourselves. This void in culture is noticeable, in particular, among the youngest: they have difficulty learning their lessons because they are too force-fed by the digital bottle.

What can we understand from the abundance of information when we no longer know how to restore things to their original culture? Here, we take the word culture in the sense of "way of life", of a people, of a civilisation.

It appears that we judge news, particularly international news, through the distorting prism of the culture to which we belong. Information projected onto another culture, sometimes very opposed to one's own, erupts without us having the major data to judge it. It follows that the information, plastered at regular intervals by the permanent television news, makes us lose our train of thought. Because the invasion of news on the screens gives us little time to digest it, to understand it. So, we feel this nihilism of culture. It's really jerky, an ephemeral information that doesn't get to the bottom of things because of connections and reconnections.

The man constantly connected to screens is indeed at the end of true general culture. Through cultural nihilism, the end of the thinking man is taking shape. Indeed, there is a void between man and his plethora of connections to the smartphone. By leading a smartphone life, he does nothing but dissolve into cultural nihilism, thought emptied of its substance.

5. AGAINST THE SMARTPHONE HELL

Contrary to the claims of internet giants, digital technology is indeed the end of our anonymity. The smartphone makes us lose our secrets and our thoughts. We no longer belong to ourselves in our smartphone world. It is a kind of denial of oneself, but also a plundering of oneself, of one's tastes, and of one's interests by the internet giants.

Guillaume Pitron, in his book *L'enfer Numérique*, renders us a huge service by warning us against the uncontrolled use of digital technology. Everything we do is recorded in the virtual spheres of the digital world. Through billions of conversations (likes, emails, Facebook...), humanity finds itself in the era of immediacy, of the permanent present. Through exchanges at the speed of light, we are in a digital industry that reduces this world to clicks and oneself as master of everything. In this smartphone tsunami, we surf the net like on a more or less rough sea; we watch videos, read texts, and search for information. It is indeed a rather practical but not very intellectual binge.

Beware of the "tracker" used without our knowledge by operators. Often, Facebook and Google are the worst offenders in tracking internet users. Trackers collect information without our knowledge to send us abundant advertisements. The information, stolen from us with each connection, reveals something about our personal lives. Even our movements are tracked, as well as our political opinions, and our pathologies. In this sense, anonymous data is just a joke. The postmodern man is under surveillance. This is called a smartphone dictatorship that replaces democracy.

This concerns our individual freedoms greatly violated by a kind of improvised web police. This sort of state surveillance on its citizens illustrates the concept of a digital hell. With the smartphone, we are no longer free to think for ourselves, since in connections, we are provided with data to think in our place or to think in a biased way, a bit like in totalitarian countries like the former Soviet Union. In any case, our freedom depends on quite surprising digital contingencies, as everyone is under surveillance. We are almost prisoners not of the Gulag, but of the digital and big industries: Google, Facebook, Snapchat, Apple, Cloud, Tik Tok, Instagram...

Apparently, we cannot rely on the neutrality of the Web. It always takes sides as a general overseer of our digital actions. *"The internet shapes a world where human activity 'stricto sensu' is no longer the only thing animating the digital universe. Computers and objects communicate with each other without human intervention."*

We will have to adapt to this new nonsense of human history. Men talk to each other as originally; then they talk to machines, and now machines talk to us and to each other. Such a humanisation of computers comes down to putting man and the computer, man and robots in competition. To the thinking robot, let us prefer Pascal's "thinking reed" in his "Thoughts". Such human and non-human activity clearly shows the end of man, end of thinking for oneself, end of free will. It is acceptable for robots to discuss among themselves, but for robots to talk to humans, it shows a suspicious equality taking the form of artificial intelligence in competition with human intelligence (natural).[21][22]

And what will be the status of reason in the supposed dialogue between men and robots? Such a question bewilders our postmodernity. Philosophy has always operated through reason and within human reason, not within

---

[21] Ibid., p. 231.

[21] Guillaume Pitron: L'enfer numérique. Voyage au bout d'un like, éditions Les Liens qui libèrent, 2021, p. 231, Paris.

robotic reason. Reason is the faculty to think and speak. It is also common sense (the "bona mens" evoked by Descartes). It is hard to see how computers would show common sense. Here, we fall into nihilism, into nonsense. Let us reject this *"super artificial intelligence at the service of the planet"* (G. Pitron's expression).

The smartphone hell is an everyday experience: without our knowledge, social networks, conspiracy theories flourish more than ever. The digital age gives a disastrous resonance to conspiracy doctrines taking the form of conspiracy theories. Every conspiracy theory is defined by the political and economic domination of the world by an unknown group. This theory allows for blaming a population for the evils of our postmodernity. In reality, *"conspiracism is a worldview that asserts that the course of history is not the result of national political games and uncertain human actions, but that it is actually uniformly caused by the secret action of a small group of men desiring to achieve a project of control and domination of populations."*

In this context, conspiracy theories, in the form of sub-arguments, are authentic mental manipulations mainly targeting the youth. They grow up in an anti-educational atmosphere. Conspiracy social networks do not educate the youth; on the contrary, conspiracists aim to shape young people into permanent rebellion against order and hierarchy. Where are the moral and philosophical references through anti-social networks? Already, our postmodernity is in disorder, and conspiracism adds more disorder, as if to show that a world of suspicion is better than a world in search of truth.

For example, young people are raised to believe false information online. It is therefore manipulated without its knowledge, especially when conspiracists designate scapegoats without providing proof. In front of adolescents frozen on their screens, conspiracy theories go unnoticed: they do not appear in the form of labels. On the contrary, by moving forward in disguise, conspiracy theories distort the ideas of internet users! In addition to the distortion of information, there is a more formidable distortion, that of undermining free judgement and free interpretation. How can we understand that our interpretation is the result of a distortion of facts? Here lies the poison against reason; our common sense is caught in a network of nonsense, that is to say, the goal of conspiracy is to put an end to our discernment. It only takes a single doubt to criticise, to suspect past and present news. So that the mind of the young person is abused at will. This amounts to crimes against truth and reason on the part of theories that distort information. We are here in the nihilism caused by conspiracies.

Anti-conspiracy theorists and anti-conspiracsists do us an immense service by warning against the freezing of our intelligence, against mental manipulation. They denounce certain information on social networks by calling them a vehicle for a great manipulation of consciences, a rhetoric of silent nuisance. This is why we sometimes have to put our cell phones away.

Vigilant and philosophical postmodernists react against conspiracy and the distortion of stories. They unmask the sponsors behind the facts or appearances. Suspicion of historical facts, or more precisely, the falsification of ancient or recent history, is an underlying activity of conspiracy theorists, of a minority who like to tamper with the news by spreading fake news in abundance.[23]

An example of fake news can illustrate this delusional conspiracy: the idea that Buzz Aldrin and Neil Armstrong would never have walked on the Moon because, in the photo, the flag is flying while there is no air, constitutes real disinformation aimed at undermining this American feat. Historical and scientific disinformation can only harm the conspiracy theorists themselves because, by falsifying history, their lies become obvious: too much falsification kills falsification so that fake news falls into the abyss on its own, in nihilism.

These pseudo-conspiracy theories have an anti-philosophical character, taking the form of anarchy of thought and actions, of permanent suspicion. The weapons of the weak on social networks are rumours, lies, falsifications, focusing attention on subjects classified by history. Conspiracy theories, or more precisely certain tweets, certain Facebook pages, screens in general, are malicious, and "digital natives" are misled quite heavily because they only cultivate adoration for screens. So, screens become the new religion of postmoderns because they trust them sometimes naturally and blindly. This whole falsification aims to provoke an anarchy in thought: one no longer knows how to distinguish the true from the false. These two categories are mixed and sometimes neutralise each other. This is the principle sought

---

[23] Article conspirationnisme, Encyclopaedia Universalis, Paris

by conspiracy theorists, those who use screens as a political weapon, a violence. It is another way of organising the chaos of ideas, the dissolution of reference points, the neutralisation of good and evil, the hatred of others... The established order is fought against: conspiratorial screens fight against parliamentary democracy. Therefore, conspiracy theory is the postmodern form of anarchism, of a style similar to that of Bakunin! In his time, Proudhon also exalted anarchism, an ancient form of conspiracy theory.

6. THE SMARTPHONE ALIENATION

Connectionism shows a certain alteration, alienation of the smartphone man. All alienation is always passive; that is to say, we undergo an agitated life without our knowledge. But what alienation are we talking about? The alienation of work takes place in life, and religious alienation is located in consciousness. To economic and religious alienation, let us add smartphone alienation in the postmodern in its relationship to digital. Here in smartphone alienation, man is a stranger to himself and to multiple connections: he does not benefit from screens; on the contrary, he suffers from the malicious attacks of social networks and he becomes ill. Consequently, he is deprived of his life, so he becomes ill from the digital. Smartphone alienation is the digital hell in which men remain due to their nonsense.

The thesis of labour alienation can be applied to the alienation of the internet user: in the use of screens, the smartphone user no longer asserts himself but denies himself. He does not feel comfortable. He believes he is happy in hyper-connectivity, but in reality, he is unhappy because his mind is ruined. He would be better off without the smartphone, but he does not know it. In the alienation of the mobile phone, we find the notion of nihilism: the numerous connections are contacts in the void. We are here towards the end of man thinking for himself.

We are amazed by the daily passivity of young and old people in front of screens since their reason is almost neutralised: reason becomes mad because it no longer plays its role of reflection; in front of screens, reasoning is anaesthetised. So, we are led by connections and by a natural and automatic will to continue to connect anarchically to see ephemeral images and writings...[24]

---

[23] K. Marx: Le Capital (1.XXIII)

The internet user forgets that he is no longer himself in front of the screens; he is perfectly alienated.

In fact, digital alienation (the Cloud, big data or mega data, artificial intelligence, the internet) shows that users are like different, artificial beings, so that their own intelligence no longer serves them. They are sometimes aware of their state of alienation. To alienate is to make other, to be other, that is to say, to be a solitary living of infinitely multiplied connections. The exponential nature of the digital creates a real dependence, an addiction despite oneself, even though one did not want to fall into this smartphone addiction. However, we are sick of living in hyperconnectivity: it becomes a daily need so that the smartphone user becomes one with his phone. I remember a teacher confiscating the mobile phone of two students because they were constantly connected in class. So, the two students took out their glasses case and started tapping on it as if to show that they needed a substitute for their phone, thus showing their addiction to the smartphone.

The alienation of the smartphone lies in the absence of humanity in the digital world: relationships are falsely human on social networks. Our postmodernity takes the form of a materialistic cybermodernity, since our relationship to the digital is very neutral. We have moved from a fairly human existence to a rather disembodied digital existence. There is a true digital culture here, taking the inevitable form of digital materialism.

Let us appreciate Milad Douhili's formula: "the digital has defeated the body." This could mean that the digital and the human body (in some of its aspects) form a somewhat dubious and dry unity. Indeed, the digital experience is a sensitive experience, an experience of personal sensations. The osmosis between digital and body goes through the sensitive touch of the keyboard; then, seeing the screen, it is feeling a second time. These sensations are those of images, screen size, and unlimited connections. Digital sensitivity takes the form of materialism, of a material life. Digital sensitivity, according to Antoine Vidalin, replaces the flesh since in the digital world, man becomes a "matter that denies itself." That is to say, in front of digital screens, where are the true human relationships? Where is real fraternity? Social networks do not show fraternity in action. That is not their purpose. We do not see anyone "in flesh and blood." So, virtual fraternity is very neutral, very useless. In sending or receiving an email, there is never a direct relationship, from human to human, from person to person. The email, always silent, becomes a correspondence without body, without flesh, without eyes, without a face. And in this neutrality of the digital, lies the end of the person, the end of man. This is indeed a very bad consequence of the death of man. This is digital alienation: "man is denied," and therefore I am no longer flesh in the use of the digital, but I am a digital being subject to the digital. That is why we are truly in the nihilism of the body: the relationships between man and the digital struggle to find meaning. The digital does not give meaning to our existence because we spend more time on screens than with humans. We will have to learn to use the digital and direct it towards the human: let's humanise the digital. For example, "videoconference" meetings are palliatives as during the Covid-19 pandemic, but in no case, this kind of distant meeting, without real exchange, will replace direct contact around a table.[25][26][27]

"Never before, in the history of humanity, has such an experience of brainwashing been conducted on such a large scale."

Sabine Duflo:

"When screens become neurotoxic, let's protect our children's brains."

Hachette Livre, 2018, p. 230, Paris

---

[25] Milad Doueihi, Frédéric Louzeac: Du matérialisme numérique, Hermann, 2017, p. 56, Paris.

[26] Antoine Vidalin: Personne. L'existence numérique ou la négation de la chair, Artège, 2021, Paris.

[27] In 2018, in Hamburg, children protested in the streets against their parents and asked them to put aside their mobile phones and, furthermore, take care of their families. This protest against the selfish behaviour of parents shows that children are giving them moral lessons: when a home is created, one is expected to take care of their children instead of spending exclusive time with the mobile phone.

CHAPTER 3

SCIENTISTS WARN AGAINST THE EFFECTS OF SCREENS - HYPERCONNECTIVITY, THE DISEASE OF THE POSTMODERN ERA.

1. CRITIC OF THE DIGITAL FEEDING BOTTLE.

In our postmodernity, we have seen that the homo sapiens has become the constantly connected but very disconnected man from human relationships, from physical presence with others. His way of turning only to his disordered connections shows a disruption in methods of discussion through screens... This reversal is not in favour of a philosophical relationship. Indeed, this kind of disembodied relationship reinforces our agonising postmodernity. In his disconnection from his surroundings, the screen enthusiast strives to prolong himself in often suspicious and practically useless smartphone relationships. Do true human relationships need to go through disembodied screens? It appears that loneliness in front of the smartphone is hardly felt; however, one is truly alone in constant connectivity, in its illusory relationships.

We live with difficulty in the frenzy of connections and disconnections. Are we truly happier in this exercise of focusing our attention on the smartphone? That's why, let's take a test to measure the time spent on our smartphones, thanks to the author of the "Digital Bottle:"

"You have a maximum of 5 minutes to read."

You must only count and remember your number of 'yes'.

Be decisive in your answers; it's either yes or no! In other words, no 'maybe' answers...

The deliberately reductive use of the term 'internet' implicitly implies all activities connected on smartphones (social networks, online games), and more generally, all activities connected to the internet.

If you want to propose it to your child, adapting it in a 'familiar' version will certainly be necessary for better 'contact' between the young... and themselves.[28]

1. *Do you often feel preoccupied by the internet (thinking about your last online activity, or your upcoming evening online session)? Preoccupied)*

2. *Do you feel the need to browse the internet for increasingly longer periods to be satisfied and 'fulfilled'?*

3. *Have you tried repeatedly, but unsuccessfully, to limit, control, or stop (on your own) your internet usage Control)*

4. *Do you feel tired, exhausted, depressed, or irritable when someone tries to limit or stop your internet usage? Nervousness)*

5. *Do you stay on the internet longer than you initially planned? Exceeding*

6. *Have you put at risk or are you at risk of losing a significant relationship with a friend or someone close due to internet usage?*

7. *Have you ever lied to your family (or your wife) or to other people in order to have more time to use the internet?*

8. *Do you use the internet to escape and avoid your problems, or negative emotions (abandonment, guilt, anxiety, depression)?*

There, you have finished reading and conducted your own analysis. Enough joking around: How many 'yes' answers did you tally?"

From how many yes are we addicted? For the scientist Kimberly Young, an American researcher, a pioneer in warning against overconsumption and disrupted connectivity, five yes make the internet user a "potential sufferer of

---

[28] Stéphanie Blocquaux: Le biberon numérique, op. cit., p. 88-89. This book is practically useless because it sheds no light on our digital postmodernity and its harms.

internet addiction." Contrary to the claims of S. Blocquaux, there is indeed an addiction here; that is to say, an unsuspected suffering, a dependence on the smartphone somewhat similar to alcoholism. Here we are talking about "net addicts," that is, those who are unable to do without screens, habits that cause suffering if hyperconnectivity continues and if one suddenly stops looking at screens.

Efforts are made to propose controlling one's connections or digitally detoxifying oneself. For example, through self-management of connected time, one could ask a young person to write down their smartphone or digital consumption per week, especially on weekends, during school, and non-school periods. These palliatives do not encourage digital detoxification. The awareness of personal excesses in connections is often exceptional, and the resolution to correct one's excesses is often overlooked. The solution would be to delete the mobile phone or only use it for making phone calls. The use of the computer would be reserved for emails, research... We have rightly mentioned school dropouts during Covid, but we refrain from talking about mobile phone dropouts because this attitude is non-existent. Both young and older people are fascinated by connections without ever increasing the exercise of intelligence: the digital pacifier wreaks havoc on the soul.

Personal journals broadcast on screens are an overexposure of oneself on a global scale. This shows something unhealthy because one feels obliged to tell one's life, to narrate oneself.[29]

One becomes aware that the photos and phrases on social networks condemn our image and reputation without our knowledge: by displaying oneself infinitely, one believes to honour oneself, to serve one's interests. On the contrary, the continuous exposure of oneself only darkens our person and our future. Infinite profiles take the form of an overestimation of oneself. This feeling of omnipotence is only an unhealthy illusion.

The inventors of digital technology do not aim to educate man. On the contrary, violence, hatred, and fake news are served to the youth. The charlatans of Facebook and YouTube are incapable of protecting young people from violence on screens. How can one create idiotic video games like

---

[28] Catherine Price: Lâche ton portable! Programme de détox digital, Librairie générale française, 2018. Paris.

"Hatred"? Where is the protection of the youth? We are all responsible for the misuse of smartphones and the excessive activation of digital applications in young people because they are hardly taught the right methods to use the internet.

The whimsical author of the "digital pacifier" (page 178) dares to criticise the scientific truth about mobile phones according to the beautiful study by Michel Desmurget: "The Digital Idiot Factory." He even positions himself as Socrates to relativise M. Desmurget's truths about the harmful effects of the smartphone. He then shows through his book, "The Digital Pacifier," that he has not at all become aware of the dangers of screens for young people. His unconsciousness is that of an adult always tempted by the disrupted consumption of the smartphone. While such hyperconnectivity pushes a whole generation of postmodern men and women into the abyss of unintelligence. To think for oneself with others, we do not need an intermediary called the unleashed smartphone. S. Blocquaux hardly asks for the phone to be put away, that is, to be set aside for a while. He goes even further by proposing tools for virtual training while seeming to forget the drifts in undisciplined smartphone use. Certainly, he helps us fight against forms of cyber violence, but he overlooks the true education on the phone. Is it possible to educate on the smartphone, on its reasonable use? A question that is always difficult because no one can regulate smartphone enthusiasts. For now, it seems difficult to control the excessive connections. That is why one must put away their phone by personal decision. This does not mean that everyone will limit their connections by reason, nothing but reason and all reason. We would have liked the promising title "digital pacifier" to mock this thirst for disorderly and therefore anarchic connection. And finally, that this author shows the infantilisation, the irresponsibility of men in front of screens. S. Blocquaux hardly proposes to save the youth, for example by cutting off smartphone connections for the youngest from 7 pm to 10 am. Who will enforce this authoritarian disconnection so that young people prioritise their schoolwork and human relationships?

Hyperconnection has become one of the diseases of postmodern men. We know that our already sick postmodernity hardly needed any more contamination: overexposure to screens turns us into connected robots. Our postmodernity, as we have seen in our first two volumes, is already overwhelmed by the conflicts of reason and the temptation of irrationality. So, we add another irrationality: the uncontrolled use of the mobile phone, an illegitimate hyperconnectivity. The smartphone and the multiplied connections have never contributed to better living in community, to talking more, to listening attentively, to speaking to calm tensions, to dissolve the chronic violence of men, to reject honours, money, and glory. In reality, the smartphone does not give us another vision of man at all; it leaves out the human, morality, justice, and reflection.

2. YOUNG PEOPLE HYPERCONNECTED TO SCREENS: MICHEL DESMURGET'S CRITICISM

From the beginning of his valuable work "La fabrique du crétin digital," Michel Desmurget is surprised that doctors, psychiatrists, paediatricians, and journalists praise screens; they "radically ignore the effects, the dangers on young people" in the excessive use of the mobile phone. This ignorance was still relevant in 2019.

Faced with this illegitimate hyperconnectivity, we can say: Keep away your mobile phone. This "Keep away your mobile phone" hardly means break your mobile phone but become aware of the silent ravages caused by multiplied connections on the brains of young and old. And try to connect directly with humans to live better together.

We will never thank Michel Desmurget enough for denouncing the dangers of screens for young learners. Faced with the deification of the mobile phone by young people, one can profitably read Michel Desmurget's scientific studies: "La fabrique du crétin digital: The Dangers of Screens for Our Children." Notice the analogy of this text with that of Jean-Paul Brighelli's "La fabrique du crétin.". These two alarming titles point towards the end of the education of man. On this point, Brighelli denounced the lack of work, the end of concentration in class, in a period that was not entirely marked by the evils of the mobile phone. We find the end of the instruction and education of man in the use of screens, all on a ground already deprived of rigorous and attentive studies. So that the void of education before mobile phones, associated with the void of education in the time of mobile phones, leads to the end of man, the death of man. In this context, screens, which we have known for a long time, do not advance general culture, human relationships, and the education of the postmodern man.

What are the effects of the multiplied use of screens on the brain, especially of young people? We finally have a serious study that dramatically answers this question. Here, we recall the fundamental points of "La fabrique du crétin digita."

1. The duration of screens is an overtraining for the under-education and non-education of man. Desmurget provides frightening figures on screen consumption time:

- School children between 2 and 8 years old consume 3 hours a day of screen time, which equals 1000 hours annually. They spend a quarter of their life on the mobile phone.

- School children between 8 and 12 years old: 4h45 = 1700 hours annually. They spend 1/3 of their life on the mobile phone.

- High school students aged between 13 and 18 years old: 6h45 per day = 2400 hours = 40% of normal waking time = 100 days = 2.5 school years. They spend 40% of their life fidgeting on their mobile phones.

These figures come from scientific studies. By screen, we can understand television, internet, Facebook, Twitter, Instagram... The most ardent are high school students: 6h45 of screen time per day, or 2400 hours annually. This amounts to two and a half years, the equivalent of the hours of second, first, and final year classes. This is time forgotten to prepare for the future. Time spent on screens is time lost for learning lessons. In the past, when there were no mobile phones, young people also wasted their time in front of the television or at festive outings. Today, these 2400 hours are truly hours of dramatic solitude, of confinement in a digital prison: where are the true human relationships? Nothing beats direct contact by disregarding screens during discussions. We then witness the end of humanity, and therefore the end of the education of the postmodern man.[30][31][32][33]

The digital does not strengthen (moral) education. Mr. Desmurget's studies confirm this educational impasse.

So, young people hardly practice self-education in their anarchic contacts on the web. Indeed, solitude does not educate; the constant viewing of screens constantly distances us from any form of education of man. And what do young people remember from their 40% of daily time consulting their mobile phone? Not much, it seems, because they are too bombarded with information. Only disconnecting from the mobile phone or occasional connection will bring a real life; that is, to put away the mobile phone and talk to others, get to know others.

Here are the other harmful effects of screens:

2. Intelligence and functioning are the first victims, as well as the impact on language development, because children no longer pronounce words and no longer interact with their surroundings (page 269).

3. There is a depletion of vocabulary because screens do not elevate the mind in terms of general culture (Page 266).

4. Screens show the absence of real sharing and direct exchanges. Moreover, they are a source of difficulty in concentrating on something else and a waste of time.

5. Screens, "it's great": this formula is a myth and a falsification of true discourse and the education of the young.

6. The false "digital natives": children learning to write on a keyboard have difficulty memorising a lecture, recognising letters, and reading, while those who learn with pen and paper know how to read and do not confuse letters.(Page 231)

---

[30] Michel Desmurget: La fabrique du crétin digital. Les dangers des écrans pour nos enfants, édition du Seuil, 2019, Paris.

[31] Jean-Paul Brighelli: La fabrique du crétin digital. La mort prochaine de l'école. Éditions Jean Claude Gawsewitch, 2006, Paris.

[32] Alphonse VANDERHEYDE: La fin de l'éducation de l'homme? Volume 2 of the Acquis de la mort de l'homme, published by Connaissances et Savoirs editions, 2020, Paris.

[33] ibid., p. 197.

7. "The more we abandon a significant part of our cognitive activities to the machine, the less our neurons find material to structure, organize, and wire themselves."(Page 231)

8. Screens interrupt the continuity of our nights, so sleep is constantly disturbed(page 142).

9. Children connected indefinitely to screens are threatened for their intellectual development since their blood circulation is affected... (page 304). The young person will be psychologically impacted by the plethora of hours spent sitting in contemplation of screens.

10. Video games do not improve students' intelligence (Page 145).

11. Young people barely sleep five or six hours a day because they are too much on screens. Regularly disturbed sleep deteriorates the brain: when we sleep, the brain sorts and classifies information like memories. Sleep stimulates growth and fights infections. "The body is therefore repaired." (Pages 296-297)

12. Avoid screens before going to school and before sleeping.

13. The class without a teacher is a myth (page 242). The MOOC phenomenon is a lure (page 245). The Massive Open Online Course (MOOC) offers courses on the internet. It is often just course videos; sometimes there are evaluation tests and discussions among participants. All of this can be sanctioned with a certificate of competence. Students need teachers with direct contacts. It is, therefore, false to claim that MOOCs allow us to do without school. Learning on screens at school is equivalent to not learning anything (page 245).

14. Screens are a silent assault on our health. They can promote the following diseases: obesity, anorexia, bulimia, smoking, alcoholism, drug addiction, depression, sedentary lifestyle... Because of screens, we sleep less well. The use of digital tools before sleeping causes incomplete nights (5 hours for an adolescent who consumes 4 hours of screen time per day, when they should sleep 8 hours or more).

15. Digital technology does not resolve the differences between privileged and disadvantaged students (page 235), so the intellectual level does not rise much.

16. The Internet is an illusion of available knowledge. Just because Google asserts it, doesn't mean it's true, especially since websites provide documents written by ignorant individuals with false or stupid statements.

17. Screens follow an economic logic. The pedagogical logic is highlighted, but according to M. Desmurget, it is a deception. It is true that domestic screens offer a scientific, "clear, coherent and indisputable" reading.

"The more students watch television, play video games, use their smartphones, and are active on social networks, the more their grades plummet. Even the domestic computer, endlessly praised for its educational power, has no positive impact on academic performance. This does not mean that the tool lacks potential virtues. It simply means that when you give a child (or a teenager) a computer, unfavorable recreational uses quickly outweigh educational and formative uses." (page 252)

Here is M. Desmurget's opinion on screens for educational use:

"Here again, the scientific literature is unequivocal. The more states invest in information and communication technologies for education (...), the more students' performance declines. The more time students spend with these technologies, the lower their grades. Collectively, these data suggest that the current digitization movement in the education system is driven by a logic much more economic than pedagogical [...]."(Page 253)

18. Teachers are the most important resource in schools (PISA). Placing a (struggling) student in front of screens will not help them fill their gaps. The teacher will never be the software but the professor: it is nonsensical to introduce competition between digital and teachers. The mobile phone is an anti-educational tool par excellence. Those who exchange SMS during a high school or university class compromise their studies and retain the course less well than those who pay attention and concentrate during the class. (Page 241). Mobile phones should be banned in high school, and those who bring their mobile phones inside the school premises should be sanctioned. Let's ask them to put away their mobile phones, leave them at home.

Facebook, Netflix, Snapchat, YouTube, Instagram, are they really invitations to increase our knowledge? (Page 239). Common sense is the least shared thing in the world by robots and artificial intelligences. It is the end of wisdom, the end of human education, the end of thinking man. Why do they often connect? It appears to be an irresistible temptation for postmoderns, and they have the illusion that hyper-connectivity is true human connection. In reality, we deceive ourselves with each connection. Let's write that screens are the new religion of postmoderns, but a religion that poisons them unknowingly. We can never listen enough to scientists about the dangers of screens, of this anarchic contemplation. The philosopher will never write enough about the trivialisation of the mobile phone, its uselessness for the studies of young people. Michel Desmurget's analyses and warnings provide the greatest service to doctors, psychologists, teachers, educators, parents. But would it still be necessary to listen to Desmurget's lessons? Are connected adults capable of it? Or as usual, do they prefer to succumb to ease: say nothing, offer their children the latest model of a mobile phone? Is this the education of the postmodern man?

Here, the scientist Desmurget is engaging in moral philosophy work as he denounces the harmful effects of screens. Such lessons fall on deaf ears among mobile phone enthusiasts. They refuse any criticism of screens because, for them, the mobile phone is sacred. This sacredness is not religious; it is rather neo-pagan in a context of the end of man. Screens keep man in his finitude: the smartphone directs man towards his end. Common sense or wisdom no longer concerns humans in their relationship with screens.[34]

As we have said in our previous research, man is already in a civilisation's end. With the mobile phone, it is a confirmation of the end of our world. Is there a way out of this end of civilisation? An exit is possible if the adults who bought the mobile phones for the young people turn to reflection and reading alarmist books on the thoughtless use of screens, on this denunciation of illegitimate hyper-connectivity. Let them turn to screen disconnection or moderate screen use, the only way out for postmodern men. Do we want to educate children, instruct them, or give them a mobile

---

[34] Gaspard Koenig: La fin de l'individu. Voyage d'un philosophe au pays de l'intelligence artificielle, Le Point, 2019.

phone to have fun? However, the adult who gives a mobile phone to a 5-year-old child is ignorant of the harm to the brains of the youngest.

After reading Desmurget, let's write that scientifically, screens are a bad acquisition from the death of man. For more than two centuries, we have been in this death of man. It was believed that screens would be a progress in humanity, and therefore they would have shown wisdom in their use. But the screens arrived in a postmodernity already very suffering and agonising. The screens suddenly precipitate our civilisation into the unknown, into the abyss of the end of man. Adding nothing to nothingness is to remain in the era of emptiness, in a postmodern end of civilisation. Let's note here that for the first time, this end of civilisation also concerns other cultures. Moreover, in China, in India (...) the mobile phone also wreaks havoc, especially among the young. But here, these countries do not know the notion of the death of man as we have seen in our previous researches.[35][36]

---

[35] Alphonse Vanderheyde: La fin de l'éducation de l'homme? Volume 2 of Les Acquis de la Mort de l'Homme, published by Connaissances et Savoirs Editions, 2020, Paris.

[36] Alphonse Vanderheyde: La philosophie de la mort de l'homme, Volume 1 of les Acquis de la mort de l'homme, published by Connaissances et Savoirs editions, 2017, Paris.

CHAPTER 4

IS THE SMARTPHONE EGO HATEFUL AND DICTATORIAL?

This famous formula, "the ego is hateful," is inscribed by Pascal within Christianity: the ego is proud, constantly seeking glory, one of the baseness of man. It is not a question here of making us horrified by our being, but of avoiding exalting our ego. In the Pascal sense, the ego is self-love that "becomes the centre of everything"… It is unknown to others in the sense that it wants to enslave them because each self is the enemy and would like to be the tyrant of all others. The ego is hateful hardly means a self-hatred against oneself or a self-hatred by our interlocutor, but of a true unhealthy self-love.

The ego, transposed to the smartphone, is even more hateful because it becomes an icon of oneself, self-admiration, self-satisfaction, and self-power. The ego shines in front of everyone and infinitely through the photos and messages sent on screens to the public, that is, to the whole planet. Certainly, in our overconnected postmodernity, the ego has a national and international resonance, but why such a univocal vision of oneself? By surfing on screens, everyone transposes their ego much further than their home. This outrageous ego would be called selfism, self-branding, or self-promotion, regardless of the names given to the power of the ego, to self-idolatry. The ego is "iconised" by itself: screens amplify this living iconisation of oneself. This amounts to vulgar narcissism and a great waste of time.

Umberto Eco has already warned us about the amplification of the ego on screens. Because in the past, in newspapers, a few were highlighted, but in the smartphone era, anyone can glorify themselves, spreading their words (often insipid) throughout the entire world. Every home has become a global village. Consequently, the words of the insignificant, of the ordinary man, become an almost universal word and almost equal to the celebrities of politics, music, and sports. So, there is a confusion of words, a comparison always suspect. This explains the numerous friends (often unknown) of the mobile phone.

The ego becomes a sort of "contemner" of the body. This ego-contemplation is the new religion of the smartphone man: to contemplate oneself is to admire oneself, and this self-admiration by oneself takes an exponential form. In essence, most of the screen users only seek to show themselves: one goes from self-contemplation to the contemplation of the self by others. In this sense, this unhealthy double contemplation would naturally encourage putting away one's mobile phone, especially since this kind of activity contributes neither to good human relations nor to public discussion, but to a constant withdrawal into oneself, playing constantly between me and myself.

The ego is therefore hateful in our postmodernity in the sense that making oneself the centre of everything is to adore oneself, while cutting oneself off from others. And we hardly see the point in constantly exposing ourselves on the web as if we were very important. And what should we do with the others? Because the ego does not exist without others. The relationship between me and the smartphone still remains dry. Because, in the end, we spend more time looking at our cell phone than talking face-to-face with others. Therefore, with the ego exposed, over-exposed, one must keep away his mobile phone and take it out to use it when necessary, in order to avoid the over-cluttering of the smartphone ego.

The power of the ego generated by the cell phone is an illusion. It seems that self-admiration does not bring full satisfaction. The images of oneself on the web are only distorted dreams making one believe that one is important. So, there is a false situation of the cell phone, a false opinion of oneself: the overvaluation of one's self makes one lose contact with the reality of what one is. Pascal wrote that "man is the toy of deceptive powers." In our postmodernity, the ego is fragmented; it is the victim of this deception by the attractiveness that the cell phone exerts on other consciousnesses. In reality, we are unconscious of the damage caused by self-care: the ego has an inauthentic pressure to control the world when it is hyperconnected. It is a sport that is neither intellectual nor physical.[37]

Today, the deceptive powers appear in the form of a conspiracy of the ego with itself, of certain contents (images and writings). As a toy of deceptive powers, man falls into vanity. He is deceived by himself. The ego is, in itself, a deceptive power when it projects itself onto its mobile phone, when it invades its smartphone with images of itself. This is indeed narcissism, a contemplation of oneself in several copies ad infinitum.

This is where we can better understand Pascal's formula: "the ego is detestable." It is important to be careful not to fall into the often suspicious, unhealthy narcissism that shows a certain lack of self-esteem. The numerous intrusions of the ego through photos and profiles are like acts of coercion: we forcefully show ourselves to everyone. This lack of modesty is embraced by the "contemptors of the body." Between the detestable self and false friends, there is an unconscious analogy of identical "Selves" seeking meaning in their lives. And the "detestable self" finds meaning in the free platform of the smartphone.

The power of the smartphone self, under changing profiles, manifests a certain dictatorship of images, since the constantly sent photos impose themselves and clutter social networks. We do not ask to receive images every day. The smartphone is, first and foremost, a refocusing on one's own life. Outside of the ego, nothing is important to the smartphone user. Therefore, the individual using their phone has unwittingly founded a totalitarian system with its connections, texts, readings: screens are a danger to the self because this self becomes tyrannical.

With the smartphone life, we are far from this formula of Epictetus: "cultivate self-government". Instead, the mobile phone user erects his ego as a dictatorship while surfing on social networks. How proud to be seen, to be constantly seen (have you seen me?). Nothing brings consistency to the multiplied ego because it is a disordered ego, always in disagreement with itself. Social networks have already had 20 years of harm, of withdrawal into oneself, or more precisely, 20 years of self-dictatorship through digital means. For example, the phone has become extremely useless, extremely

---

[37] Blaise Pascal: Pensées, Le Livre de Poche, 1995, Paris, paragraphe 455, p. 209.

depersonalised; it is the cover of a misplaced or misplaced life in pathological hyperconnectivity. The dictatorship of the self through social networks is established in our lives...

The ego swells when it goes on the phone because it has free access to all documents, to all social networks. But this adventure, of planetary vision, will never make the individual a reflective being. On the contrary, he will be a despot exercising imaginary domination over the world. Everything happens in absolute solitude in front of screens. Formerly, as today, one thinks of oneself, of glorifying oneself, of enlarging oneself, of showing that one occupies a central place in this life. One is almost famous, one believes, in the self-manipulations of profiles. One even keeps an intimate diary taking the form of a temporary narrative of one's life, often without great philosophical interest.

Every diary shows his moods, his worries, his cries in the face of what is considered unjust, violent. And what is surprising is the increased invitation to "like". First of all, these "likes" are forced and give the profile too much importance to me. We practice a dictatorship of the self when we ask to "like", when there is no debate, no dialogue. Often, these are "likes" by instinct and not by reason. For example, the personal journal becomes global and, in this case, do "likes" have any real meaning?

The like is a constant test of popularity. We look for the like as a notation of the power of the self and as a guarantee of the lies on the web. These likes, often thoughtless, invite a furtive glance at the smartphone and attract often laudatory comments. We find ourselves here in a sort of struggle with our own personality.

In the digital postmodernity, we fall into the search for our popularity rating, whereas it is a bulimia to be cured by reflection. Social network users are victims of the smartphone illusion, of addiction, of the narcissism of the like, of a dictatorship of the self. The deification of oneself in front of everyone is a fault that becomes positive under the gaze of a few doubtful internet users. While the main thing is elsewhere than on his temporary profile. The need for recognition and self-esteem propels us to display ourselves in front of everyone. It is then a question of self-idolatry, self-deification, and the search for glory, "the greatest baseness of man."[38]

The like has no sense since it means nothing. Contrary to the assertions of Eric Sadin 39, this logic of like does not follow the triple obligation of giving, receiving, returning. We hardly see where the gift through like is. Invoking the theory of Marcel Mauss in his "Essay on the Gift", is this really another way of showing that there are social relations through social networks? But Mauss' problem concerns the exchange of gifts and feasts in primitive tribes: when we receive a gift, there is an obligation to return another gift, otherwise we are bound and we contract a debt. Where are the real exchanges on the web? Where are the real friends who share your concerns and whom you meet in their homes and not on screens? Here in the smartphone, it is hardly a question of gifts sent and received with an obligation to return. It's about gifts that poison the web. We have nothing to say in the face of the flood of images, of profiles in our already drifting postmodernity. Facebook does not distribute gifts. We are hardly obliged to receive, to return the likes, that is to say to put a like and a positive comment which is often succinct.

How did we come to take care of our profile by changing it and changing it again? Our postmodernity has become entirely "image", photo, self-portrait always flattering its "ego". The responsibility of producing profiles falls on digital creators, but also on those who use their phones to show themselves and receive flattery.

In reality, what does a photograph on a mobile phone consist of? According to Roland Barthes, *"the photograph does not necessarily say what is no longer, but only for sure, what has been"*. Boring images on Facebook, Instagram, Snapchat, and Discord are scourges of our postmodernity. Their users hardly know that every photo, every profile is already in the past. In reality, a photo is never in the present, always indicating what is no longer. Every profile is an illusion, but behind this flattery, there is what Freud calls "the instinctual need to assert oneself". It is a certain unhealthy self-satisfaction but always necessary when one does not value one's own person or for some to live; they need to glorify themselves because they have hardly any other personal satisfactions. But the profile shows a certain duplicity of oneself, an unfair view of one's ego. The profile makes one judge everything from oneself. Certainly, we often think of the world from our own perspective. But this culture of self isolates me from others. The smartphone cultivates a "hateful ego".

The mobile smartphone is a mirage of the all-powerful ego. Such fictional contemplation is a deception of the self. Nietzsche had already shown that the ego is a fiction: in "I think," the "I" does not think. It is in a Cartesian context of the thinking ego, of the cogito, of "I think, therefore I am," that Nietzsche contests the value of the self. As the self gets lost in becoming, it cannot be known precisely. The ego is not an "I think" because nothing is thought. The subject, the self, moves from one fiction to another, from one dubious profile to another. And the follower of these profile-changing games does not understand himself, does not know his own identity. This is indeed a dissolution of the subject or the ego unconscious of itself. The smartphone ego does not think. It is the mirage of the entire phantasmatic power of the digital. In reality, an ego that imposes itself on others through its profiles ad infinitum lacks emotional, psychological, and intellectual maturity.[38][39][40][41]

Finally, according to Nietzsche, "we are all something other than what we appear to be because of the states for which we have consciousness and words." This means that the self is a deception because it does not appear true. It is hypocritical and wants to give itself other appearances to conceal what it really is. Our true inner life is hidden beneath the positive appearances of oneself, of the gaze cast by others. The concealment of the true ego behind the appearance makes sense in portraits, self-profiles. Because we hardly have self-awareness of our actions in smartphone manipulations.

---

[38] Blaise Pascal: Pensées (pensée n°44), Le Livre de Poche, p. 179, Paris
[39] Eric Sadin: L'ère de l'individu tyran: La fin d'un monde commun, Grasset, 2020, p. 153, Paris
[40] Roland Barthes: La chambre claire, Gallimard, 1980, Paris.
[41] Nietzsche: par-delà le bien et le mal, paragraphe 16, Aurore, tome IV.

CHAPTER 5

FRIENDS, OR RATHER, FAKE SMARTPHONIC FRIENDS

Why be friends with someone? To this question, Montaigne answers that he is friends with Monsieur de La Boétie "because it was him, because it was me." True friendship is hardly explained because it is the natural result of a slow and private construction. But in our sometimes-inhuman postmodernity, are friends found on social networks real friends?

We know that the GAFAM produce more long-distance friends than real friends. Let us emphasise that social networks should bear another name. Indeed, a social network should be a network of friends: "socius" in Latin denotes companion, associate, friend. But with Facebook, Instagram, virtual friends are friends by proxy, and social relationships will never be identical to true friendship. This is why we can speak of false friends, false associates, false companions. Friends separated by a screen and whom we never see at home are hardly friends: they are simply acquaintances for a day with whom we rarely have open Socratic style debates. Digital discussion is far from philosophy because there is a need to always speak often without much reflection.

The claim to have hundreds of distant friends either shows a lack of true friends in life or friendship through a screen helps to compensate for this deficiency or to pass the time. Social networks ignore Aristotle's words in "Nicomachean Ethics": "Without friends, no one would want to live." In fact, we do not choose our family, but we choose our friends. But pseudo-friendship by proxy within anti-social networks leads to the ruin of true friendship. Friends by the dozen on Facebook are as many suspicious friends who do not necessarily want your well-being. This kind of digital friendship is very dry, neutral, and therefore indifferent to you. Smartphone friend groups are to be considered as unfaithful acquaintances, and again, it is improper to speak of friends on social networks because in reality, we do not know them, we have never seen them, we have never spent time with them. Let us not confuse the supposed friends of anti-social networks with real friends from our circle who have been interested in us for a long time. Social networks distort true friendship.

Virtual friendship is an illusion. True friendship is always in action; that is to say, it exists, and it has meaning. Otherwise, it is better to put away your phone than to correspond occasionally with alleged friends. And in the end, 500 friends and more on Facebook do not build anything with you because you can hardly talk to them in real terms. Let us select, choose real friends who support us during difficulties in our existence. It appears that false friends (this is the true name of friends from anti-social networks) appear indifferent and even hypocritical. The following words of Blaise Pascal can easily apply to alleged friends, companions, associates of anti-social networks: "We do nothing but deceive and flatter each other. No one speaks of us in our presence as he does in our absence. The union between men is based only on this mutual deception and mutual flattery; and few friendships would survive if each knew what his friend says about him when he is not there, although he speaks then sincerely and without passion."[42]

Smartphone friendship is in contradiction with true friendship, as we read in[43]

"Nicomachean Ethics". For Aristotle, "friendship between honest people is safe from slander." Friendships are based on virtue. According to Aristotle, it is a moral friendship that requires no.[44]

Written because "the essential, when it comes to virtue and morals, lies in deliberate will." 48. Now,[45][46]

---

[42] Montaigne: Essais. Livre premier, Le livre de poche, 2015, Paris.

[43] Aristotle: Éthique de Nicomaque, livre VIII, chapitre 1, Garnier-Flammarion, 1965, p. 207. Paris

[44] Blaise Pascal: Pensées (100), Le Livre de Poche, 1972, Paris.

[45] Ibid., p. 56.

[46] Aristotle: Éthique de Nicomaque, p. 213.

In antisocial networks, this thoughtful and virtuous friendship hardly flourishes. Smartphone friendships are not based on virtue, nor on utility, nor on pleasures. These three friendships, according to Aristotle, are valid in ordinary life. In moral friendship, "virtue and the virtuous man are the measure of all things", [49] because it is a being who wants to achieve good for himself and his friends. However, social networks hardly favour honesty, good, or the company of virtuous people. Certainly, for Aristotle, man, a political being, is made to live in community: "Every city is a community", that is to say without community, life is impossible for man. But social networks are hardly like a set of living communities: virtual life is, by definition, a borrowed life, an artificial life in which the GAFAM forcibly bring humanity. But precisely, where is the human? Where is the true friend-to-friend relationship?[47]

With social networks, one could say, "O friend, there is no friend." If one believes to be friends with necessarily distant internet users, it would be the end of true friendship. And one remains alone with the delusions of our smartphone. Through virtual friendship on asocial networks, the reinforcement of loneliness is at play. Because the plethora of connections takes up time, loneliness lurks since we are somewhat dehumanised. This dehumanisation wreaks havoc on thinking. Here, we are more or less like Robinson on his deserted island, emptied of the human, of the human community. The "fake friends" of the mobile phone, whom we practically never see, participate in a world without others, without feeling their real presence. Our smartphone world more or less refers to Robinsonades. In "Friday or The Other Island," Michel Tournier recounts the solitary story of Robinson lost on the island of Speranza. He's shipwrecked and finds himself alone in a world without the presence of others. He recreates "a human world," that is to say, he remains human by living from hunting, from cultivation... His great enemy is loneliness, that is to say, he lives in a city that he manages like a humanity but without men.

What would Robinson's story be like with a smartphone? Certainly, he could do video calls, talk to anyone, have infinite virtual friends; but without the real presence of others, Robinson remains more or less human. Because man needs to live among his peers to exchange, talk, and observe others.

---

[47] Ibid., p. 228-230.

While Facebook users have voluntarily chosen a smartphone life more or less away from humans, away from others, they suffer from loneliness in front of screens. If they hardly put away their phones, it is for the reason that they have chosen to embrace solitude and therefore they no longer think for themselves, preferring to remain in their endless connections. In short, Robinson has only God as his master, the followers of social networks have the smartphone as their God, but a neo-pagan God that poisons existence, because we are no longer free to think for ourselves, as we are mechanically guided to reason in a smartphone manner, that is, artificially. Let us add that the smartphonists of our neo-pagan postmodernity are very different from Robinson and his Christian world by definition. Today, the digital hell rejects everyone into isolation. And ultimately, we accept this condition of being isolated, of being without contact with humans despite the numerous connections. Are we not becoming digital Robinsons with all proportions kept, that is, to suffer from isolation and a certain smartphone dehumanisation? Let us write that Robinson is more human than the internet users of our postmodernity. All of Robinson's work is to kill inhumane time, that is, his world devoid of humanity. All the time of the smartphonists of our neo-pagan postmodernity is spent with a single "materialistic friend": the phone. And they do not seem happy, even with their numerous friends for a day. This is not the case with Robinson when he meets Friday. Certainly, at first, he is wary of him but gradually, they become friends, real friends.[48]

---

[48] Ibid., p. 141.

PART TWO

DIGEST YOUR MOBILE PHONE

CHAPTER 6

WHAT DOES IT MEAN TO DIGEST YOUR MOBILE PHONE?

Digesting your mobile phone is surely calling for a digital diet. But digesting means assimilating the abundant data from the phone in order to think about them, to rethink them. Then, digesting your phone is taming your smartphone: opening it when I have decided and not when I receive messages and other notifications. It is necessary to digest the infinite documentation contained in the smartphone. For example, for Nietzsche, digestion holds a great place. He considers that culture begins not with the soul but with the body: "the right place is the body." It is known that Nietzsche does not like morality, as it comes from the ideals of Christianity. But one is surprised by the definition he gives of morality: "Morality, that is to say affects - as identical to the organic: the intellect as the stomach of affects."[49][50][51]

This shift from the concept of morality to physiology allows Nietzsche to reject morality and its principles. He prefers to consider the human body as "a collective of living beings" and a centre of intellectual activities. Ultimately, thought is done by our body and in our body, Nietzsche was concerned with the good health of the body. He interprets life physiologically. Physiology is a discourse on the body. The stomach is the seat of physiological thought, so that thinking is indeed digesting all our intellectual activity, or as Nietzsche

---

[49] Fragments Posthumes, volume X, Print-aut. 1981, 11 [128] in the Colli and Montinari collections, p. 356

[50] Alphonse Vanderheyde, Nietzsche et la pensée bouddhiste, op. cit., p. 148.

[51] Héraclite, Fragments (translated by Marcel Conche), 62, P.U.F., 1985, p. 234, Paris

says: *"Perhaps all morality is an interpretation of physical instincts"* with good or bad digestions.

For several reasons, Nietzsche's analyses on the body and thought, the stomach and thought, the stomach and morality interest us today in our relationship with the phone. Indeed, our smartphone life is a life of the body and not of the soul. Because we experience connections bodily, digitally: we go from connection to connection, that is the plenteous digital activity. So that we think more digitally than intellectually. This way of thinking bodily explains our wanderings, the temptations to constantly connect. This amounts to living with one's phone and less with humans. However, it is necessary to think for oneself, or more precisely, to rethink and reflect on the message, the information read: the soul is not the seat of thought; it is the stomach that contains the digital reason.

From then on, our smartphone activities reveal the relationship of our body with an inert machine, with invasive screens. So, let's digest, that is to say, understand, tame, and select what we read on the mobile phone. The postmodern has a physiological relationship with his digital tool; he thinks less intellectually because he lives in the ephemeral, the illusion. The plethoric invasion of written messages causes poor digestion or a lack of digestion, so that one ends up digitally intoxicated. But thinking for oneself about the contents of the mobile phone is quite exceptional. This is where good digestion is found, that is to say, mastery of one's connected life, chained to screens.

It follows that those who think a lot are capable of digesting well, of understanding everything that circulates on the internet. At least, they try to grasp the content and scope of such information. Every postmodern is capable of reflecting on the nuisances in the plethoric use of the smartphone, provided that he takes the time to analyse the fundamental data of the digital machine. But let us remember that with the vagaries of techno-science, like the advent of the digital smartphone, we have driven away personal reflection.

Digesting smartphone information is difficult. However, we hardly suspect such poor digestion, which is nothing but an inability to digitally detoxify ourselves. Intoxicated postmoderns, saturated by their numerous connections, thus live without remedying their physiological state, their digital state. Let us become aware of the satiation of our stomach by smartphone manipulations. Let us begin to digest by ourselves, that is to say, to think. Let us avoid the digital machine grinding our reflection. On this point, Heraclitus of Ephesus writes: "Thinking well is the supreme quality."

Digestion occurs when one thinks for oneself. Indeed, digesting the mobile phone also means engaging in good activities on screens. For example, Wikipedia organises freely without the interventions of digital giants: everyone can participate in word editing. In this sense, there is no digital intoxication; on the contrary, it is good to seek to define words. Furthermore, during the 2020 pandemic, professional use of digital technology was possible at home through telecommuting: digital technology facilitated life (virtually) a little. The smartphone allowed us to remain human, to digest it better, to contact friends, to promote human relationships, to learn more about the information offerings on the internet, to speak via video, to adhere to pedagogical continuity; we hardly had a choice, we had to live and speak from a distance.

The two months of confinement in 2020 were an opportunity to think for oneself. Taking a step back from the world is necessary, including with one's smartphone. During the confinement, one could have feared a real indigestion from staring at screens for hours, but in reality, the postmodern was able to kill boredom and exercise intelligence without being disturbed by the routine of the usual daily life. Obviously, human relationships were sometimes difficult in the house. As seen in Sartre's "No Exit", "hell is other people"; in reality, hell is the absence of others, the absence of a true human relationship, even though this is always necessary for any person in our postmodernity.

CHAPTER 7

THE MOBILE PHONE AND ARTIFICIAL LIFE

1. PLATO'S LESSONS ON SHADOWS

We will never cease to reread Book VII of Plato's *La République*, especially in our drifting digital postmodernity. Socrates apparently tells this allegory of the cave (which describes a state) in a literary way within a Platonic treatise. Remember that Plato resorts to myth when reason is failing to explain our human condition; here, myth and fable refer to our quite fragmented humanity. It was already Plato's concern to understand man in his state of ignorance but also in his state of true knowledge.

Recall that Plato describes our condition as humans: we are locked in a cave and chained by the neck and feet, staring fixedly at images projected on the wall. "Here is a strange picture and strange prisoners," writes Plato. In many ways, these prisoners...

Sonniers resemble us. Some consequences of this allegory could be applied to those who use smartphones.

Firstly, these prisoners hardly know that they live in illusion, in copies. That is indeed the first lesson of this allegory. The internet user lives like the prisoner in the cave: he conspires with his dreams. When Plato denounces the vain phantoms, eyes turned towards the images, the smartphone user constantly lives with screens by checking his texts, his images. He is hardly aware of being in an unhealthy contemplation, in an addiction to the outpourings of all that is artificial. So, his life, in the shadow of his smartphone, is not very different from those prisoners in the cave.

The fixation on the images on the cave wall brings us back to an artificial life. Similarly, the smartphone user is a prisoner of screens by his own will: he prefers to endure the stuffing of images so that he is sick to the point of indigestion. It is impossible to digest plethoric images: the postmodern, with his smartphone, is sick, but he is unaware because he is one with his phone, with the screens. Therefore, his shadowy reality is reduced to that of the prisoners in the cave.

In this sense, Plato anticipates cinema. Indeed, his description of the cave can be likened to a movie theatre, and everyone staring fixedly at the images projected on the screen. This is our very artificial human condition. What can be said about our smartphone life? It is identical to that of the prisoners in the cave, and even more so, postmodern individuals are subjected to the assaults of screens to the point that their lives are lost in anarchic images: their addiction hinders them from detaching from their shadowy life. On this point, Heraclitus had already warned against illusion. "Men are deceived in the knowledge of visible things."

Another lesson we draw from the allegory of the cave is the guilty culture of the prisoners' ignorance. We live in dreams; it is the ignorance of our human condition because we are infected by endless images. Today, despite the use of the internet, the postmodern is even more ignorant at times. When navigating the net, he feels like he knows everything. We are as ignorant as those prisoners in the cave and even by amplifying connections, we become increasingly ignorant; that is, without real general culture and without exercising our reason. The maze of anarchic connections has isolated us and made us miss out on life. Certainly, the internet contains a stack of anarchic knowledge, but the smartphone user is always in a state of zero knowledge. On the contrary, he will always show that he knows things because he surfs the net. But we know from Heraclitus of Ephesus that *"great knowledge does not teach intelligence."*[52][53][54][55]

The lesson from Wim Wenders can help us understand the weariness of images, or rather, the anarchic invasion of images, the impasse in which

52 Plato: République, translated by Bacou, Garnier-Flammarion, 1984.

53 Geneviève Droz: Les mythes platoniciens, édition Seuil, 1992.

54 Heraclitus, Fragments (traduits par Marcel Conche), P.U.F., 1986, p. 113

55 Ibid., 91.

our smartphone world finds itself. Indeed, in his film, "Wings of Desire," he denounces the invasion of television images into our lives. In 1987, it was the reign of television, and postmodern individuals were already suffering from a profusion of images. Let's stop suffering, stop looking at shapeless images. At the time, we did not understand this suffering, this false education through improper images. It is because we are ignorant of this suffering that Wim Wenders shows a television without images. Imagine a smartphone without images, without text; it is another way to criticise digital screens. Do we need a smartphone diet?

It follows that the hell of images begins already in the cave and its prisoners, then in television, and finally in the digital realm. The digital hell is one of the greatest catastrophes of our inhuman postmodernity. Plato denounced in his time our unhealthy fascination with images. He warned us against the (digital) lies of images. In this context, reality TV shows fit well into the illusion: the prisoners do not play a role, they live in illusion and ignorance, but the fans of reality shows deliberately distort our world by presenting life as a game. Because they need it to exist in the illusion: they play fiction as if life were a conspiracy against their own dreams. Reality TV is not a human game, but an artificial game. It is a bit like transforming humans into robots.

This clearly shows that our smartphone world is governed by digital robots since connections are made from machine to machine (connected homes, smart cars...). There is a real strategy of destruction of the human being: we no longer have our place in our postmodernity. This is also the death of man, of his culture, of his history. Screen prisoners are automatons, robots always in connections and leading an artificial life... Some non-human activities take place on the internet; robots interact with other robots... Not to mention that emails amplify "rumours on social networks".

Another lesson from Plato's allegory lies in the liberation of a prisoner from the cave. He frees himself from his prejudices by using his reason: he thinks for himself and thus unmasks the illusion in which he lived. He breaks free from the chains of prejudices because he has become aware that his reality is shadowy, that the images projected on the cave wall are false. His liberation takes the form of a rational constraint: the former prisoner thinks for himself, makes an effort to weigh the pros and cons. We hardly see the smartphone user reject what he sees. On the contrary, he enjoys the illusion and does not seem to opt for rejecting his prejudices, for discussing with himself, for exercising his reason. However, the former prisoner acts with reason, with free reflection. For the true smartphone user, thinking for oneself also means digesting one's phone. The right place is the mind, or more precisely thought as a dialogue of the soul with itself. Thought is a kind of soul digestion, but in our postmodernity, we no longer know how to digest, that is, to think. Contrary to the former prisoner, smartphone users have difficulty freeing themselves from screens, a question that does not naturally arise. As we have just seen, this lesson from Plato also concerns postmodern individuals immersed in materialism, idolatry, and copies. Who dares today to put away their phone or to digest it? Indeed, digesting one's phone is to understand, reflect, turn away from screens with intelligent will to avoid digital intoxication, intoxication with images. Freeing oneself from one's chains is to liberate oneself from the guardianship of images on digital screens; it is to know how to use the smartphone correctly through a discipline of connection. Digesting one's phone is to use one's reason sensibly. The former cave prisoner knows how to turn away from images and become aware of true reality. Similarly, why couldn't the postmodern individual, immersed in their smartphone world, make this same detachment process from shadows, from fake news?[56]

Why refuse this effort to think differently? A sort of soul self-education is necessary; it is also another way to digest one's phone. Self-education is the self-awareness that we must think differently about our reality, about our illusions: let us encourage the postmodern individual to unmask the illusions of this world. Reject the digital pacifier or, more precisely, digest the smartphone or understand it; open it when we want to preserve our daily life. Digesting one's phone is to free oneself from the smartphone yoke; it is another way to use one's mobile device with reason and to remain master of what one writes. For example, when I write an email, words are automatically suggested by the power of the GAFAM, when it is up to me to choose them and not to the robotic smartphone! Man is not a digital robot. We will never stop writing about the ravages caused by digital screens on the young and the not so young. Everything is done to encourage postmodern individuals

---

56 Pitron: L'enfer numérique, op. cit., 232-233, Pari

to become worshippers of the smartphone. And it is the human being that we must talk about, not the robots. Man is a thinking reed, not a thinking robot.

Prisoners in the allegory of the cave are like valets leading a virtual life. Let us study Robert Redeker's thesis: for him, we live in a society of valets, for example, Facebook is the triumph of anarchy, the end of man. This takeover by social networks shows a grip on our thoughts: we are valets. The ancestors of today's digital world are shows like "Loft Story": reality TV was a kind of voyeurism, an exhibitionism showing a display of oneself to everyone. The valet is the postmodern man watching "Celebrity Farm" or "Star Academy". *"These programs are made to turn each of us into valets."* The social networks, the crowd of tweeters, of Facebook participating in the bashing of famous men. This outburst of valets shows a method of degradation, of hatred, of self-righteousness. So, the valets find their befuddlement normal, their inauthentic criticisms, those who believe they hold the truth. The valet designates the one who does not elevate his mind, who does not seek to understand. In other words, the valet is "our soul when it sleeps while our body remains awake". In this, we witness a nihilism of thought. Ultimately, the valet is the one who watches screens imagining that this is reality. In fact, it is reality TV or the digital-reality.

In short, the prisoners of the smartphone today are hardly different from those described by Plato in his *République*. However, with this difference: the prisoners of the cave are victims of illusion since they are fascinated by the images projected on the cave wall, while the prisoners of the smartphone are victims of illusion by their own fault: they voluntarily and mechanically amplify illusions through unlimited connections, and consequently, they are guilty actors of their own production of fiction. They connect constantly, automatically, and often without reflection. Ultimately, they sink to exhaustion in images and texts. Before the digital age, one could still discuss, think for oneself without intermediaries, in order to dispel illusions as the former prisoner of the cave did masterfully. With smartphone life, this exercise is truncated and even eliminated by the almost religious relationship of man with artificial intelligence and by the absolute necessity of constantly consulting his phone as if real life is found on the screens of smartphones or his computer. And with the cerebral modifications of man and therefore with the combination of man and technology, we are in a waning postmodernity and therefore in nihilism: man and thought have lost their respective meanings. Everything is inscribed and evolves in an atheistic and anti-Christian context. This leads us to an uncertain future.[57]

2. TRANSHUMANISM OR ARTIFICIAL LIFE

By constantly playing on his phone, the postmodern becomes one with it, so that when the time comes, the phone will be grafted directly into the head, and then we will play at being sorcerers. In this case, the connections will be automatic. This is already a sign of transhumanism that we can call a non-humanity: man, as we know him today, will be significantly modified by himself. We are here in a more dangerous, more infernal situation than the prisoners described in Plato's *République*. The latter remained human in their ignorance and do not claim to transform man. Whereas postmodern scientists want the end of man, the death of man through their transhumanist proposals. The computer can imitate man and his thoughts, but it will lack the organic body. However, transhumanism goes further: it wants to modify the original man.

The postmodern has invented robots that transform him, that reduce his humanity: he can become a mix: half robot, half human. He no longer controls his destiny. We are in an era of nihilistic transhumanism. We are in a permanent industrial revolution. The human part would be reduced, and therefore, man would no longer be man. He would be half technical and half living. This is no longer science fiction but an end to humanity as we know it today. This third industrial revolution will be the last of our humanity because we are moving from a human life to an artificial life.

Man is neither robot nor humanoid. Humanoid robots or android robots will never replace humans! Let us take with reservation these words of Yuval Noah Harari: *"Future technologies are likely to change homo sapiens itself, including our emotions and desires, not just our vehicles and*

---

58 Robert Redeker: Réseaux Sociaux: La guerre des Léviathans, Editions du Rocher, 2021,
    p. 35.

weapons." [58] [59]61 Man is not more man in artificial intelligence. Even if its brain could be controlled by an artificial body, does it need to burden itself with transhumanist delusions which take the forms of nanotechnologies, biotechnologies, artificial intelligence, cognitive sciences (NBIC)?[60]

Let us return to the objective reality of our natural intelligence, our human way of thinking, speaking, and understanding. Indeed, *"from a purely scientific point of view, artificial intelligence does not think, artificial intelligence does not suffer, artificial intelligence does not like."*

[61]The sacralisation of artificial intelligence poses the end of man. But this shows the weariness and refusal of the ordinary man to think. We know from Éric Weil that the ordinary man does not like the philosopher because the philosopher thinks and, above all, has a judgement on everything and everyone. The philosopher's bad reputation comes from the fact that he thinks; also, he knows what speaking means. The philosopher is certain to convince the ordinary man, but the fact is that the non-philosopher refuses to think and to dialogue among equals.[62]

Similarly, artificial intelligence does not know what thinking and speaking mean. Indeed, it would be absurd to dream of an artificial intelligence that gives us answers to every (existential) question. Where is the effort of thinking, of dialoguing to solve a problem? What is the point of entrusting our reflection to a so-called artificial intelligence? Human conceptualisation power is superior to artificial intelligences in that man is above machines. However, we are presented with the opposite option: it is artificial intelligence that will dominate natural man. The alleged idea that the machine understands mental operations faster and helps us understand

---

[60] Daniel Andler: Intelligence artificielle, intelligence humaine: la double énigme, Gallimard, 2023, Paris.

[59] Ibid., p. 34

[61] Yuval Noah Harari: Sapiens, Albin Michel, 2015, p. 485, Paris.

[62] Charles Delhez: Où allons-nous ? De la modernité au transhumanisme, Salvator/fidélité, 2018, Paris

[63] Gaspard Koenig, La fin de l'individu. Voyage d'un philosophe au pays de l'Intelligence Artificielle, Édition Observatoire, 2019, p. 63, Paris.

everything is heresy. It will never be able to explain things metaphysically and will be unable to answer the question: what is man?[63]

Reasoning, nothing but reasoning. All reasoning will always be on the side of the man who thinks, who gives a coherent speech without resorting to artificial intelligence. This illusion of artificial intelligence is the stock-in-trade of those who refuse to put themselves in a position to think, to make an effort to understand a human problem, and to solve it through public discussion.

Artificial intelligence raises the issue of superintelligence and machine assistance. For example, *"Ray Kurzweil, the American technophile guru who has the ambition to achieve immortality, to upload his mind onto an electronic chip, probably believes that thoughts float in the air."*

Here, Kurzweil's atheism is part of our neo-pagan world. Never will any infernal machine (by definition) solve the problems of the community. We will always have to go through discussion, or else we will be in a civilisation change: it will no longer be a human civilisation, but a humanoid, hybrid, artificial civilisation where feelings and emotions will have disappeared.

For a long time, many philosophers have been writing about the end of our civilisation, the death of man. This end of civilisation means that something else is possible, but it is a neo-pagan world that opens up before us, and that we live in an atheistic and profane way. The conditions have been met since the digital age, especially with its representative, the mobile phone, for man himself to disappear, more precisely for him to transform, to get lost in so-called artificial intelligence. It appears that AI is linked to transhumanism. However, the very frightening transhumanist project is found in these words of Charles Delhez:

"Today, technosciences and biotechnosciences open unsuspected horizons: increasing the cognitive capacities of the brain (...), creating two-way interfaces, brain/computer or brain/brain, allowing computers to read the electrical signals of a human brain (...). There is also consideration of manipulating memories and diving into virtual worlds."

In the future, could we mentally send messages to other humans? In April 2017, "Facebook launched a programme to directly decode our

64 Éric Weil: Logique de la Philosophie, P.U.F., 1990, Paris.

thoughts in our brain and transcribe them into an SMS message." This is indeed a deception, a trick, as if we can communicate telepathically. Are the transhumanists taking us for fools? All this shows that nothing makes sense when we want to modify man. In the future, will man be a cyborg, a hybrid being, part human, part robot, being modified by metallic or silicone grafts to improve his cognitive performance?[64]

We are already connected to objects (pacemaker). Amputees undergo grafts with biochips connected to the brain... it is progress in humanity. But as soon as we move to mental manipulation, it is the end of our postmodernity.

What arrogance to want to modify our lives through technology (rejuvenation, increase in intelligence through biology, abolition of suffering)! Let's go back to the natural, Darwinian man, as opposed to nanobiotechnologies. No robot will reach the level of consciousness (morality) of man. Only man has consciousness; he has rights, duties, feelings, emotions... To eliminate all this is to merge into permanent nihilism, into nonsense, into absurdity, into a postmodernity that has lost its meaning and human values...[65]

The sorcerer's apprentices, like the cyborgologists and the transhumanists, are part of a new sect whose object is mental manipulation. Thus, digital technology contributes to mentally manipulating the minds of the young and the not so young. Its actions are very similar to those of a sectarian group: the sect of false scientists convinced that humanity must undergo a transformation of its being. It cannot be emphasised enough that it is necessary to understand and digest what has been happening for the past 25 years with digital technology and to warn against the next 25 years of a modification of our humanity, of the substance of what makes a human being with articulated language, with values, beliefs... In our postmodernity, let's continue to think without artificial intelligence. Because the essential thing is to understand our world absorbed in a transhumanist drift: man becomes God.[66]

---

65 Ibid., p. 95.

66 Nietzsche: Ainsi Parlait Zarathustra, op. cit.

    Michel Foucault: *Les mots et les choses*, Gallimard, 1988, Paris.

67 Charles Delhez: *Où allons-nous?* op. cit., p. 114-116

The postmodern scientist seems necessarily atheistic and even against all religion. He no longer makes a distinction between the sacred and the profane because he ignores the sacredness of man made in the image of God. Therefore, he is outside of theology and the sacred words recorded in the Bible. The doors are open for humans to manipulate since he knows neither the forbidden, nor moral conscience, nor what is sacred. He has therefore easily taken the place of God on earth.

The man's claim to compete with God is a poorly posed question. Indeed, behind alleged scientific advances and digital progress, transhumanism does not present itself in divine terms but rather atheistic. Paradoxically, the atheist man takes himself for God, but a god made for atheists. The transgression of Adam and Eve is hardly an issue here with transhumanism. Disobedience to the laws of God is no longer the problem of our postmodernity. Transhumanists will not naturally utter this formula from the Bhagavad-Gita: "Now I am become Death, the destroyer of worlds." These words were cited by Robert Oppenheimer on July 16, 1945, after the explosion of the first atomic bomb. Oppenheimer is of Christian faith. He appeals to the sacred, to a religious word known to compensate for the destructive consequences of the atomic bomb.

Transhumanism is part of disenchantment. Transhumanists are not against the atheistic creation of this world. Therefore, we are indeed in an end of man, in an end of human history, in the death of man. In this sense, transhumanism is indeed a bad outcome of the death of man.[67]

---

[68] Jacques Arnould: Quand les hommes se prennent pour Dieu, Forum/Salvator, 2020.

CHAPTER 8

THE CHALLENGES OF DIGITAL ETHICS

1. POSITIONING THE ISSUE OF DIGITAL ETHICS IN OUR NEO-PAGANISM.

Our digital postmodernity navigates without ethics: it is hardly the major concern of postmodernism. Yet, the use of the internet requires us to assume responsibilities. Faced with the invasive digital realm, we are not yet petrified by the misuse that some make of endless connections. Every day, we are concerned with ethics, say ordinary, usual when we perform actions. But with the digital, actions go unnoticed because they involve digital functions, typing on a somewhat dry keyboard that does not immediately raise ethical questions.

Through the anarchy of connections, especially emails, notifications, and fleeting readings, the postmodern does not immediately realise the importance of a tweet. For example, Trump used to play, send tweets, and even encourage his supporters to take over the Capitol in January 2021. His account was suspended. In this sense, digital ethics should question the sender of tweets.

Our neo-pagan world is already in multiple crises, as we have seen in our previous research. Through its misuse, the digital realm adds an ethical crisis. In reality, it has come in a context of the end of civilization, of a careless era, disrespectful of moral laws and true Socratic style debate. This is why, for the past 25 years, the digital realm has functioned anarchically: sometimes the rules of humanity, moderation, reflection, and respect are excluded. Because our postmoderns no longer want to obey moral laws. We have seen that flawless and sinless morality, without guilt, is the norm. Let us add that the absence of the sacred, of a regular life, contributes to the harm of our postmodernity. Today, we no longer have the right to think differently from the neo-pagan majority. And if we think differently, we are isolated and excluded, even though we are only reflecting away from prejudices and the dictatorship of new pagan norms like letting everything happen without saying anything, waiting for problems to resolve themselves, giving a wide space to empty speeches of truth... There is already an ethical crisis here. So how can we build a digital ethics on shifting sands? It follows that our postmodernity, dominated by (scandalous) press, by areligious or anti-religious thought (especially when hitting hard on what is Christian), has lost its sacred references inherited from the ideals of ecclesial Christianity. We cannot emphasise enough the neo-paganism of postmoderns: they have too quickly set aside Christian culture and therefore live in a rupture with a certain Christian morality. This separation still causes them suffering today, notably in the neglect of proposing a general ethics, a moral of life (a digital ethics)...

"Rule of action: never hesitate, stop, or retreat in the middle of an action, whatever happens. Never start an action without having spent a long time facing the possible consequences (all the responsibilities, etc.)." 69

The rules of action prompt us to consider digital ethics because the internet should not absolve us of responsibility for our actions through our smartphone use. Smartphones can lead us to disregard ethics, as enthusiasts often neglect to regulate their online interactions and content.

Indeed, the digital universe is too anarchic; that is to say, without ethical reference: we do a little too much of what we want by consulting deformed information. Digesting texts is difficult, but if we turn to digital ethics for the postmodern, we will better digest our smartphone consumption.

The animal hardly poses its actions, nor its responsibilities. Only man cares about the good, that is, ethics. Now, ethics (Greek term "ethos") having the meaning of customs, habits, traditions, is a matter between oneself and oneself. The reasonable man refuses to act without principles, moral rules. Now, morality (Latin "mores") also refers to customs in the sense of choosing between good and evil, right and wrong action. Digesting one's phone is, first and foremost, acting morally in the digital domain; then it is to perform acts in accordance with ethics, that is, philosophical. The ethical problem in the digital world does not find its place because we are in a world that is silent and devoid of humanity.

2. DIGITAL ETHICS AND INDIVIDUAL ETHICS: ONE ETHIC OR TWO ETHICS?

Digital systems would be endowed with a very autonomous ethics. Such surprising autonomy is programmed by digital giants. But ethical problems are mainly human, even if two ethics coexist in our smartphone life. Indeed, it appears that ethics is about man and machine, and therefore man in his relationship to digital technology. It follows that digital technology, in its use, refers back to man, to his double digital responsibility, that is to say, to the design of digital technology in the "workshop" and its practical use. The immediate data of the smartphone naturally raise ethical questions, then our personal practice on screens. What actions do we perform when we type on our keyboard?

Digital tools manufacturers are primarily concerned by ethics. But we know that their field of definition is trade: their concern is financial, very honourable when it comes to creating jobs. However, they cannot refuse some good behaviour in their digital programme. Do they regret their smartphone inventions when they have noticed for 25 years the misuse, by internet users, of certain social networks that we have described as sometimes antisocial networks? GAFAM are responsible for the excesses of certain digital users, for example, when screens are flooded with fake news, hateful messages, and surveillance of our choices... Why is there not systematic self-censorship by broadcasters (GAFAM)? Ethics arises before the commercial giants of the internet, particularly in the protection of data, in the transparency of platforms and algorithms. For example, the principle of non-commodification of personal data. By carrying out this commodification, without our knowledge, it is another way of guiding our tastes, our interests, of controlling ourselves, of monitoring our actions and gestures. In this sense, the digital ethics concerning the GAFAM alone is difficult to pose in our amoral postmodernity, that is to say that the fault is no longer primary, it has even disappeared. By these anarchic methods, the

GAFAM bring us back to the law of the jungle, to strict control of ourselves and our way of consuming. We cannot trust the "autonomous" digital system with prefabricated ethics. How can ethics be activated without man? Remote ethics are always suspect. Because it does not clearly accomplish what is expected of it without human assistance. Basically, ethics firstly concerns man and his reason, then digital technology equipped with artificial intelligence. In reality, at the base of GAFAM, it is the man who is in question, he is the person responsible for digital ethics. We hardly see this responsibility put into action behind digital anarchy.

Digital ethics and the ethics of the smartphone machine constitute two moral responsibilities shared between GAFAM salespeople and humans using the internet. The question of whether such a smartphone machine can think is important because postmodernism has had the effect of humanising digital technology, but this human-machine is often opposed to the human-human. In this sense, today, there would be no question of two entirely separate ethics, but there is only one ethics since ultimately, it is man who makes smartphones, who programmes and who plays on the net. Only humans become aware of the usefulness of natural ethics in handling the smartphone because they have a moral conscience, unlike a smartphone machine which only accomplishes what is asked of it.

Contrary to the positions of Catherine Tessier, we affirm that a digital programme is indeed concerned by ethics.[71] There would be a first ethics, that of irresponsible digital concepts. For example, why wouldn›t the GAFAM automatically cut off the mobile phone for elementary, middle, and high school students from 7:30 pm and only allow 2 or 3 hours of connection per day? Do we want to save young people from the nuisances of the mobile phone? It will be said that it is the parents› responsibility to limit the use of the mobile phone. In this sense, there is indeed an ethical and educational behaviour towards children so that they succeed in their schooling and not just succeed in beating digital screen time records.

If on one hand, ethics belongs, in a certain sense, to the GAFAM, on the other hand, smartphone users are more individually concerned by the sometimes-harmful use they make of their screens. Digital ethics unfolds in a legal, but also individual, approach. We can have all the laws against the misuse of smartphones; the essential thing is the individual in their easy and unconscious relationship with digital screens. We are responsible for what we write quickly and immediately on smartphones.

3. DOES DIGITAL ETHICS RAISE THE ISSUE OF INDIVIDUAL FREEDOM?

Digesting one's phone is managing one's freedom of connections and disconnections. We are free, and sometimes we do not know what to do with our freedom. According to Kant: "the history of nature begins with good because it is the work of God, the history of freedom begins with evil because it is the work of man." This history of freedom is first the story of Adam and Eve. They hardly knew how to manage their freedom because they believed that freedom does not relate to any law. However, God forbade them to touch the tree of knowledge. The transgression of the Lord's law is a temptation too great, because one believes to be alone with their freedom. However, as we know from Rousseau, there is no freedom without law. In essence, it is the law that guarantees freedom! There is no total freedom to do as one pleases according to one's emotions. The individual has the possibility to choose between the good act and the bad act. While not ignoring the nature of the bad act, each person chooses to act according to their instincts, their advantages, and not according to reason.[68][69][70]

In this context, the question of digital ethics and individual freedom in our postmodernity arises. Hannah Arendt saw that freedom results from will, that is, it depends on us, on our choice.[73] Therefore, digital ethics is a question of individual will. Because our will can choose good but also evil. Choosing good means being reasonable, moral, thoughtful, and just in the daily management of our smartphone. It is to write wisely on our screens, to use digital technology as little as possible (except for work), to feel free to respond or not to an email, or to open our phone without constraint. I look at my phone when I want to and not when there is a notification. Otherwise, we are slaves to digital technology. It is easy to succumb to the temptation

71 Pour une éthique du numérique par le comité national pilote d'éthique numérique, P.U.F., 2021, Paris.

72 Kant: Conjectures sur les débuts de l'histoire de l'humanité, Le Livre de Poche, 2018, Paris.

73 Hannah Arendt: La liberté d'être libre, Payot, 2019, p. 52, Paris.

of being constantly connected. Glancing constantly at smartphone screens leads to idleness. We can hardly focus our time on screens and perform any task correctly because the conditions for seriousness are not met since the phone is the first concern.

Digital ethics refers to our freedom, to the management of our actions. No one can think for us, yet the smartphone tries by all means to influence us, to guide us. We are under surveillance in freedom. So, digesting one's phone or using it, becoming aware that this digital tool is made for those who know how to manage their freedom, that is, manage their applications with discernment and question a certain way of behaving: behind freedom, it is always about the man having the final say on the information disseminated by digital technology. On this point, our freedom obliges us to analyse, to understand the abundant data of the phone. This could be called empowerment and responsibility. Digital freedom engages us in this vast adventure of understanding or misunderstanding digital technology. For example, one bears a serious responsibility when giving a phone to a 5-6 year old child. Allowing them to use applications endlessly is no longer about the child's freedom, but about a crime against youth, especially when aware of the damages of screens for children. And what does the child retain from freedom and its use? This question hardly arises in the child because they are not yet ready to exercise their freedom without learning it from adults. Furthermore, they do not have the time to think about what they see on screens. Only the adult manages their freedom; they digest their phone in the sense that they must be responsible for its use.

Never has a man using digital technology been so free to work as he wants, first by the access code to the always secret computer, then to search and surf the web. Such navigation shows the freedom of the postmodern man. In this sense, our postmodernity has an additional dimension: computer freedom, the freedom of connections and disconnections. This is where we can talk about digital ethics, that is, an ethics that refers to my freedom to act on the internet.

This power of almost total freedom would, to some extent, amount to a return to the state of nature, so criticised by Hobbes. Here, this state of nature is the state of wild digital, that is to say, anything goes on the web, spending too much time. The chaos of the internet quickly becomes the law of the jungle, that is to say, the law of the strongest, the most violent, the most contemptuous in the use of writing on the keyboard. There are also a multitude of fake news circulating on the digital. In this, it is the law of the jungle: the strongest defame the others. Finally, this state of nature teaches nothing, does not elevate the mind, and does not build any human relationship.[71]

In addition, digital ethics raises the issue of the just and the unjust. Indeed, ethics comes from the individual, from their tradition, from their culture. Everything rests on the just or unjust individual. For example, through an analysis of the just and the unjust, Plato, in his "Republic," shows that if the individual is unjust, the city will be unjust. Justice in the individual must be equal to justice in the city. Indeed, a city will be just if the individual is just. Here, the individual and the city are inseparable. Similarly, the freedom of the smartphone user and the freedom of the GAFAM must conform to justice. It seems that neither the internet giants nor the "smartphonist" individual know how to be just, that is to say, to use freedom reasonably. The just and the unjust pose our freedom through good and bad actions. It is known that bad actions clutter the digital realm (cyberattacks, scams...). This is why true digital ethics must permeate our connections. On this point, the National Committee on Digital Ethics, created in 2019, attempts to propose a reflection on human relationships in the digital realm. This committee raises good ethical questions through some contributions, some concrete cases.[72]

4. BEING FREE, IS IT ALL ABOUT SORTING THROUGH DIGITAL INFORMATION?

In our postmodernity, we are too informed. And first of all, are these digital pieces of information true, well thought out, and moral? It appears that a constant bombardment of information leads to digital and cerebral

---

74. One of the great challenges of our postmodernity is self-learning in the use of the digital device. Ultimately, it is up to each individual to control their freedom in the use of the digital tool: spend more time with our loved ones, rather than on the phone. Self-isolation is not individual freedom, but a digital prison forged by oneself and by the GAFAM.

75. *Pour une éthique du numérique*, coordinated by Eric Germain, P.U.F, 2021, Paris.

intoxication. Information is often confused with culture and knowledge. In reality, our smartphone world burdens us with subculture. Let's sort between what is useful to read and what is a waste of time and digital intoxication. Where is the ethics of information, especially in the constant advertisements that disturb our discernment and our reflection?

Over-information can lead to "infobesity". Indeed, where is the ethics when we inform too much and repeat the same information in the form of digital bombardment? Such violent methods result in making us adhere (unwittingly) to a certain way of thinking, of digesting the invasive information. So that we are prone to "misinformation", disinformation ("distorted information with the intention to deceive"): photos, videos, books appear as true. When listening to certain television channels, we expect a relevant analysis of current events, but in reality, the informants present their convictions as belief, dogma, truth. From there, it is evident that ethics is very useful as it shows its necessary presence throughout the actions of GAFAM and digital media. There is an impression that journalists and other contributors are indispensable through their supposed sacred words. Never have we spoken so much on screens, but often without real ethics, without sincerity. Digital ethics arises when we speak and write wrongly and across, when we want to reduce and denounce fake news.

It is very difficult to sort through information that takes the form of a cerebral bombardment accompanied by journalistic or specialist comments; they often show that they know everything through their often-suspicious comments. On this point, in his audience on 26-08-2023, Pope Francis denounced disinformation and fake news as the first sins of journalism. According to the Holy Father, there are four sins in journalism: "disinformation; when a journalist does not inform or informs poorly; slander (sometimes used); defamation, which is different from slander but destructive; and the fourth is the love for scandal."

It follows that it is already difficult to be honest in the information provided by professionals, so it is not surprising that in the digital world, it is even more difficult to stay ethical. As professional ethics struggle to exist, digital ethics follows the same path; that is, the path of postmodern nihilism. Because our contemporaries live alongside ethics, they have excluded obedience to moral rules because they abhor mentioning life in terms of religious or philosophical morality.

5. STRANGE SUBMISSION OF HUMANS TO THE DIGITAL WORLD: THE ABSENCE OF ETHICS.

The question is not whether social networks manipulate humans, but why do we passively accept this multiplied mental manipulation and therefore become slaves to screens? This good question is posed by Louis de Diesbach. Add that digital ethics is forgotten in servitude to screens.

In reality, there is no reason to check your phone ten times a day. And so, we hardly realise it because we have become slaves to screens to the point that we forget conviviality, attention to others... The causes of daily activations are explained solely by the denaturation of the governed, that is, internet users, and therefore by their voluntary servitude. With the digital world, we are not in a comedy but in inevitably unconscious automatisms: the fascination of images in abundance is one of the plagues of postmodern society. In the past, opponents were monitored; currently, we witness self-surveillance with the dissemination of personal data.[73]

It seems that self-admiration and self-congratulation partly explain the human desire to live smartphone or digitally: perhaps this is voluntary servitude. It is indeed the smartphone users who accept servitude through a personal decision in the use of digital screens. In this case, individual responsibility or moral responsibility is engaged in the turbulence of life through constant smartphone consultations. It is too easy to rely on involuntary, automatic smartphone habits of man. Certainly, social networks lead us into anti-philosophical illusion. But that is not the question: we are guilty of enslaving ourselves in digital operations.[74]

If the fragmented self is a weak spirit, it is because our consciences are weak and we accept to play on screens. Humans here present limits: their weakness of spirit, their life in smartphone illusion, their crushing by their lack of morality and digital ethics, their submission to the standardisation

76 Comité Pilote d'éthique numérique: Pour une éthique du numérique, P.U.F., 2022, p. 45, Paris

77 Louis de Diesbach: Liker sa servitude: Pourquoi acceptons-nous de nous soumettre au numérique? FYP éditions, 2023, Paris.

of the world; that is, there is no longer room for those who think against moderate use of digital technology. As Stephen Zweig says, it is "the opinion of all" that chooses our world and its way of life in the shadow of mobile phones. There is no longer room for originality, for those who think differently from the many. On this point, we know from Heraclitus that the crowd of many do not think, do not have sagacity.

It is the habit that needs to be noticed in digital use. This causes a trivialisation of the smartphone. Is it normal to use it more than a hundred times a day? This is a bad habit because one no longer thinks about their actions, for fear of being excluded from those who think like everyone else out of habit and automatism: where is the autonomy of reason? Therefore, the ethical question in digital use arises individually. But this is already forgotten in ordinary life: the position of actions is excluded.

But also, continuous viewing of digital images causes self-blinding to what one sees: one looks mechanically. Some are complicit in this state, in this loss of thinking, of reflection on our smartphone way of life. For example, the whimsical author of *Homo Deus*, as a fortune teller, coldly explains what homo sapiens will be, that is to say a perfect being not knowing disease, death, suffering. However, we always have to write the future, but here, it is written in advance: this leaves no room for a digital morality, for a humanism against transhumanism and posthumanism. It is observed that Harari falls into what the neo-pagan postmodernists seek: pleasure, absence of death... It is another way of reducing today's human as well as tomorrow's to an automaton, to a hybrid being without reflection. Therefore, with this book "Homo Deus," the author keeps humans in servility and even in the absence of autonomous reflection since one will think through artificial intelligence.

The submission of smartphone users to their device is explained by their lack of regulation of screens. Indeed, the question of digital ethics is carefully set aside because the postmodern is the heir of a faultless morality: guilt no longer exists. Holder of absolute freedom, he does what he wants with the new technologies at his disposal for a true transformation of humanity; for example, transhumanism excludes ethics because it is too associated with human conduct without technology. With transhumanist technology, humans metamorphose into a hybrid being: half human and half machine. While digital ethics should be the domain par excellence of transhumanism.[75][76][77][78][79]

- Dr. Hesnard: La morale sans péché, P.U.F., 1954, Paris.

- Jean Lacroix: article «Le point de vu d'un philosophe», in Morale sans péché, Cahiers n°11, Recherches et Débats, Fayard, 1955, Paris.

This rejects ethics, God, morality, fault, sin, transgression, and obedience to God's commandments (Bible). He no longer thinks in the categories of Christian doctrine but in the categories of the neo-pagan-anarchic doctrine in ideas and in the forgetting of ethics. Hence, the difficulties in establishing a true digital ethics.

---

78 Étienne de la Boétie: Discours sur la servitude volontaire, Flammarion, 2016, Paris.

79 Stephan Zweig: L'uniformisation du monde, édition Allia, 2021, Paris.

80 Héraclite, Fragments, op. cit.

81 Yuval Noah Harari: Homo Deus: Une histoire du futur, Albin Michel, 2017, Paris.

82 Paul Ricoeur: Morale sans péché ou péché sans moralisme? Revue Esprit, 30-09-1954, Paris.

CHAPTER 9

DIGITAL CULTURE, A DIFFICULT DIGESTION

1. IS THERE A REAL DIGITAL CULTURE?

Culture is the way of life of a people, of a civilisation. More precisely, culture is everything that elevates the mind through the frequentation of arts, literary and philosophical works. But can we speak of culture when we look at screens every minute? Because one wonders what elevates the mind in the computer and the mobile phone... One would tend to write that looking at screens is a very positive act, an act of contemplation more or less useful. But looking closely at social networks (Instagram, Facebook...), there is no serious general culture, a priori. So, is there really a digital culture? Certainly, for reading the news, consulting cultural sites is possible. But the definition of digital culture is difficult. For example, in some colleges and high schools, the use of tablets is quite common. The students

"Read" their books directly on the screen. This allows them to avoid carrying books in their school bag. Today, we know that digitising books does not increase students' education. Digital textbooks are rarely consulted by students. They prefer to look at Instagram; the temptations of dispersion are such that the school tablet is far from fulfilling its functions. At least with manual books, the student focused on one subject at a time... It was believed to be a great service to the students, but in reality, it was seen that they know even less than before the digital revolution.

Let us remember that the digital age was born in a postmodernity already in crisis (crisis of religion, crisis of education, crisis of the economy...). Hannah Arendt had already warned against the crisis of culture, but she

71

did so in a non-digital postmodernity. Thus, on the ruins of neo-pagan culture, the digital revolution is taking place. With the digital, one could have believed that a neo-smartphone culture would emerge. In reality, with the digital, are we witnessing a sub-digital and planetary subculture, a disappearance of general culture? Because ultimately, what remains of our infinite connections? Almost nothing. This is also the illusion of digital culture.

One could have believed that the offer of digital culture would be a major source of information disseminated in multiple subjects: sports, news, exchange of photos, texts... but the drama of digital culture lies in the fascination with shapeless images and videos. So, true general culture tends to disappear. Only fragments of culture, without much philosophical interest, remain. For example, exchanging photos on Instagram does not constitute general culture in any way. This digital culture is quite poor. Smartphone users, through their infinite connections, cultivate ignorance. It follows that they are not sick of learning on the web, but of artificially contemplating screens. In this sense, they receive too much information. And this information never forms a true digital culture.

The use of plethoric connections by smartphone users hardly leads to learning or the elevation of the mind. Thus, digital culture, a disorderly culture, causes indigestion: to be or not to be on one's phone is not the real question. It is rather: what do we learn by constantly focusing on the smartphone screen? We learn nothing. In fact, digital culture is not true knowledge, but a dispersion in the fragmentary reading of immediate data from smartphone information. Under the expression digital culture, the illusion is given that one learns something useful, that one increases one's knowledge. Even if one learns all one's life, plethoric connections weaken knowledge and the exercise of reason. We are consumers of knowledge, but the digital man consumes screens; he is not a cultivated being in the sense of Allan Bloom's definition cited above. He is rather an "ingester" of disordered information that makes him more or less sick. So he does not know how to digest the sum of what he sees on the screens, nor how to classify or sort the data. Instead of digesting his phone, that is to say, "controlling it", he ingests the information and falls victim to smartphone indigestion. Moreover, after each disconnection, he confuses what he has seen and is unable to remember the essential to promote direct human relationships.[80]

The question "Is there a digital culture?" is wrongly asked because "de facto", digital technology is an access to education and culture, but there is no real cultural purpose in the connections. It is rather about using the digital for professional use, but it is used as a toy. It follows that the problem of digital culture lies in its use: it is used for something other than cultivating oneself. There is this impression that the postmodern must always be connected to his smartphone and that this connection passes for authentic culture. It is rather curiosity and, as a result, a waste of time when there are other more interesting activities: public discussion and consultation of paper books.

We no longer cultivate ourselves by reading a good paper book. We no longer quite know the classics of literature, philosophy, and history. The smartphone deprives us of this direct knowledge. The postmodern does not read anymore; he looks at insipid photos and texts. He no longer takes the time to write since he lives in the immediate; he immediately responds on social networks without any analysis. In reality, he lives in haste with his smartphone.

A tweet, a text message, an email, are hardly part of a rigorous writing style. Our postmodernity is in cultural and spiritual distress. The internet hardly encourages learning or acquiring culture. More precisely, Google does not necessarily educate. What remains of a fleeting search on the internet? Digital technology unwittingly provokes a hatred of culture and a struggle against true general culture. It would seem that postmoderns experience an impossibility of cultivating themselves or digesting their phone. Their refusal of culture comes from their tiresome searches on the internet. They no longer digest general culture, and they reject true instruction and real learning.

---

[83] Allan Bloom: L'âme désarmée. Essai sur le déclin de la culture générale, Julliard, 1987, Paris.

2. IS OUR ALGORITHMIC CIVILIZATION A CIVILIZATION OF GENERAL KNOWLEDGE?

As Pierre Giorgini and Thierry Magnin say, *"we are in an algorithmic civilisation"*. *"But can we make sense of this? First, Larousse defines the algorithm as a set of rules or operations whose application allows to solve a problem stated by means of a finite number of operations"*. To understand the functions of the algorithm, let's first see what the mathematician Aurélie Jean thinks: she writes this,

"I am one of those scientists who try to advance the knowledge of the world. With others (because science is always a collective adventure), I developed a mathematical algorithm to model and simulate the shape of carbon particles in rubbers, in order to better understand the springs of their elasticity. For 2 years, I used these same numerical simulations to improve the technique of generating an 'in vitro' heart muscle, a technique that may one day overcome heart transplant rejections."[85]

Let's compare with Bernard Chazelle's definition: *"An algorithm is a sequence of instructions to be followed meticulously to achieve the desired result through a series of simple and boring steps. These instructions often combine in the conditional (...) These algorithms read, write, and erase without understanding anything"*.

These three definitions of the algorithm do not radically oppose each other. It appears that we are in an algorithmic civilisation. Thierry Magnin wants to establish the ethics of the algorithm, but that is not our purpose here. However, the place taken by digital and techno-sciences poses new issues such as truth, the place of the human, and algorithmic ethics.[81][82][83]

Indeed, algorithms are not neutral. The algorithmic civilisation consists of artificial intelligence and transhumanism. So, we are in a kind of anthropological rupture, whose harmful effects will be measured in the long term.

---

[84] Pierre Giorgini, Thierry Magnin: Vers une civilisation de l'algorithme? Bayard, 2021, Paris.

[85] Aurélie Jean: De l'autre côté de la machine, édition de l'observatoire 2019, page 15, Paris

[86] Statement quoted by Thierry Magnin, op. cit., Page 91.

The algorithm is a mathematical concept, but with our postmodernity, it becomes like a deity, a fascination (unbeknownst to us). For example, algorithms modify our behaviour when we watch a movie: when we turn off the screens, the algorithm suggests watching other movies. So, the algorithm is designed to increase clicks and to stay awake in curiosity. In this sense, it is not a culture, but a means to acquire an artificial culture that is forgotten instantly, it seems. Algorithms also relate to social networks and do not provide any culture? Let's take the example of Aurélie Jean, heiress of Mark I, one of the first computers built during World War II. From Mark I to today, there has been a gigantic digital revolution with inventions like Google, the web... But mastering computer language does not constitute a general culture in the school or university sense or in the sense of someone who is cultivated, who has learned, who learns for the pleasure of knowing. Certainly, a numerician like Aurélie Jean shows that there is scientific culture behind the uses of algorithms, for example, using a mathematical algorithm to model and simulate the shape of carbon particles in rubbers.

In our digital postmodernity, we are no longer necessarily driven by this need for culture, for everything that elevates the mind. We are in an algorithmic civilisation, perhaps synonymous with ignorance, with not knowing. Let us recall that a search on Google does not necessarily constitute a general culture. Because this kind of "culture" is dissolved. Our algorithmic civilisation is a forced culture without personal and critical ideas: it is an encyclopedic culture that we will never possess. Because the meticulous learning of data is lacking as we undergo what is in front of us on the screens.

The postmodern, computer adept, no longer needs to learn, since he has, at every moment, an intrinsic knowledge provided by digital tools. So, he absolutely does not digest digital knowledge. He draws from the computer his "knowledge" at any time. Thus, the effort to learn and to memorise becomes useless. Unbeknownst to us, our lives increasingly depend on the digital. We are led to lead a disjointed life.

An algorithmic civilisation raises ethical questions rather than questions of general culture, since it involves a loss of our humanity through the epistemic revolution by modifying humans (brain implants, artificial neurons, genome modification...). Excessive digitisation leads to the abolition of judgement and consciousness. As a result, algorithms impose themselves as a superior machine, crushing humans.

The algorithmic civilisation, emerging before us, is above all a neopagan civilisation, that is to say a world without God and without humans. Since both have died in ideas. Indeed, digital technology erases humans and God, and existential questions are no longer asked. All spiritual life is stifled by excessive screens. Because we are in a civilisation of poor digestion: we find ourselves alone with our smartphones, so that we live in an artificial world that we do not necessarily seek to understand. The algorithmic civilisation makes humans artificial beings who do not know how to put away their phones or even less how to digest them, that is, to understand them in their harmful effects. A civilisation of algorithms is a civilisation of transhumanism: a being half human, half machine leads us towards the end of the postmodern human. This is why a civilisation of algorithms is a bad acquisition from the death of humans, the more we advance in our artificial humanity, the more humans disappear. It follows that the connected human becomes an artificial human and the civilisation of algorithms is synonymous with a civilisation of mind manipulation. For example, Facebook manipulates all our emotions at its will.[84][85][86]

With the internet, we are in a logic of confinement, dumbing down, depersonalisation, and standardisation of consciousness. Differences are fought against, and similarities are always sought after so that unique discourses are excluded because the smartphone obliges us to think like everyone else90. Therefore, we suffer from permanent indigestion. So, will it be necessary to put away our phone, or digest it, understand it?[87]

---

[87] Charles Delhez: Où allons-nous? De la modernité au transhumanisme, édition Salvator / Fidélité, 2018, Paris.

[88] Charles Delhez: Où allons-nous? De la modernité au transhumanisme, éditions Salvador-Fidélité, 2018, Paris.

[89] https://www.technologyreview.com/1/528706/facebook-emotional-manipulation-study-is-just-the-latest-effort-to-product-users/

90 Gaspard Koenig: La fin de l'individu, éditions de l'Observatoire, 2019, p. 151, Paris

CHAPTER 10

THE ISSUE OF OUR HUMANITY - WHAT ARE THE HUMAN LIMITS?

"This future man, whom they tell us scientists produce, in a century no more, seems to be in revolt against human existence as a gift from nowhere (secularly speaking) and which he wants, so to speak, to exchange for a work of his own hands[...] This is a fundamental question that can scarcely be left to scientific professionals, nor to those of politics."91

HANNAH ARENDT

1. THE HUMAN LIMITS: DEFINITIONS AND ISSUES.

2200 years ago, the wise Ben Sira asked the following question: *"What is heavier than lead?"*. We can answer that the fool, the one who is not initiated into philosophy, the one who moves away from our humanity through his bad actions, is heavier and coarser than lead. The fool is the one who speaks absolutely incoherently, but also the one who takes himself for God through his techno-scientific inventions and therefore aspires to blissful immortality, to eternity through transhumanism and posthumanism. But also, technology, a purely human invention, allows the destruction of our world, our nature, our humanity. It is like an axe in the hands of a criminal, as Einstein said. This raises the limits of the human and a definition of man in the epic of transhumanism.

In other words, setting the limits of the human being is defining who he is and what he wants to be, and what he must not exceed under penalty of dissolution, collapse of his humanity. Would he still be entirely human, what will his identity be especially after the transformations of his body by technology? (If a man's head is grafted onto another man, would he not lose his head?). To go further, let us bring more clarity to the concept of limits. Indeed, a limit is not a boundary but a threshold imposed by the mind from within and not from the outside: nothing obliges the human being to change, to become a slave to digital techno-scientific. It is a question of marking its limits, that is to say a demarcation line between what is human and what is not human, what does not belong to our humanity or what belongs to our wounded humanity. Can we go beyond the limits? Is crossing this threshold positive for the human being? Is our reason going too far in what is called progress or the harmful effects of techniques?[88]

In another sense, limits raise the moral question as in transhumanism, that is to say, what is the future of the human being, his thoughts, his philosophy, his emotions? In particular, are we still fully human when we become a cyborg? Have we entered the era of transhumanism, that is to say, the end of our pure humanity with the advent of an artificial humanity because of artificial intelligences? It follows that setting the limits of the human being shows that the human being tends to transgress the laws of nature, the laws of our humanity, the laws of the demiurge, the universal creator, that is to say, that excess (hubris), excesses in techno-scientific research largely raise the question of our humanity, of the human being increasingly exposed to change and to modify nature, to perhaps build an uninhabitable world.[89]

Defining the limits of the human being is determining the traits that constitute man, that is to say, the human being. Who is he? What remains of his humanity in our postmodernity, a drift for 200 years, since the death of God, since man took himself for God and rejected transcendence, the sacred?[90]

---

[91] Hannah Arendt: Condition de l'homme moderne, Calmann-Lévy editions, 2020, Paris, p. 35.

[92] The Book of Ben Sira, le sage ou le Syracide (22-14) dans La Bible de Jérusalem.

[93] Alphonse Vanderheyde: La philosophie de la mort de l'homme, volume 1 of Les Acquis de la mort de l'homme, published by Connaissances et Savoirs editions, 2017, Paris.

2. WHAT IS MAN?

We know from the Greeks that they became aware of man and his proportions. For example, Sophocles evokes man as the greatest wonder of nature. Rarely has a people been so aware of man. For example, the riddle of the sphinx poses the need to think about man in his totality, even if he walks on all fours in the morning, on two at noon, and on three in the evening. This riddle of the sphinx has the merit of showing the importance of man in his animality because the human being is always an animal but speaking and thinking about the self, the world, and God, which is not the case with "other animals" (Aristotle's expression).

Similarly, the sophist Protagoras places man at the centre of all discourses. The metaphysical principle of the world is no longer water as with Thales of Miletus or fire with Heraclitus, but man. Protagoras's major thesis is man as the measure of all things, of things that are and things that are not. This also means that man is the subject and object of all discourses: every time man speaks, he speaks of himself, and it is he who holds the discourses about himself and the world. With the advent of the digital age, especially the foolish project of transhumanism, will man always speak of himself or of another man, an artificial man with human feelings but who is not fully human? What becomes of the human being and his discourse about himself opposed to the transhuman, the fruit of techno-sciences?

We owe it to Protagoras for putting man in the first place in nature. This awareness of man may have allowed Kant to discover the fundamental question of philosophy: what is man? And we will never be able to fully answer this question. We will always have to seek the answers. Because man is everything, he is contradictory, he wants, he does not want. According to Michel Foucault's studies in "The Order of Things", Western philosophy has taken man as the subject and object of its studies. Man is studied rigorously. Postmodernity is the first to think about man (almost in its entirety). The humanists of the Renaissance, the classical rationalities have given a privileged place to man, but they could not think about man, his finitude, his past. Classical thought has thought about man from the finite since he is bounded, he occupies a place in the order of the universe, he is free, but today we think about man as the object of all studies and as the will to subject the universe to his yoke. As man is the object of the human sciences, he is a very recent invention (19th century) while being under the threat of disappearance, of death (of man).

What is man? This is a question addressed by psychology, sociology, history, psychoanalysis, and philosophy. And now, today, science in its digital form encourages us to redefine man based on its studies, notably transhumanism, with an upheaval taking the form of a new man (so we believe), of a quasi-android, of a being half robot, half human both physically and cerebrally: are we witnessing a manipulation (of man created in the image of God)?

It follows that in our postmodernity, the question "what is man?" is obsolete: with techno-sciences, we question the transhumanist, that is to say, the modified man. So it is no longer man that we will question; we will no longer draw our knowledge from man but from the trans-human or the trans-human. Therefore, the new question around which our postmodernity must work is this: what is the trans-human? Does he remain fully human with his artificial intelligence, his hybrid body, half robot, half flesh... This is a change of civilisation: we are entering the neo-pagan era of the transmuted man, of the man with artificial intelligence who claims eternity and therefore immortality. And man, how far will he go to escape his human condition and enter into an ahuman or inhuman condition? But we will be careful not to substitute the question "what is man?" with the question "what is the digitised, artificial transhuman?" Because the second question has no philosophical meaning and is in total contradiction with Kant's philosophy: we will always seek to understand and explain what man is and not his transhuman substitute, which belongs to illusion. However, we seem to be heading towards a world where man will be excluded and where questions will no longer make sense. Will we be in a human nihilism with techno-sciences?[91]

---

[94] According to Hegel, in other lands, people confuse human and animal proportions; for example, in Egypt, Horus has a falcon's head and a human body, and in India, Ganesh has an elephant's head and a human or child's body.(cf. Hegel: Leçons sur la philosophie de l'histoire, Vrin, 1987). Paris

3. THINKING ABOUT THE HUMAN LIMITS IN THE DEATH OF MAN AND GOD

The human and its limits are an ambivalent theme in light of the dual expression "death of God" and "death of man". It is contradictory to think about the limits of the human in "the void of the disappeared man." If man is dead, how can we still discuss him? Or do the techno-sciences of our postmodernity question the place of man in nature and in the universe through experiments on humans, through the desire to create a new man? Will he still be fully human and fully emotional, sensitive, and thinking by himself?

As we have already seen in our volume 1 of "Les acquis de la mort de l'homme", after Nietzsche's announcement of the murder of God by men, our Western culture is disturbed. It is in a civilisation's end. "God is dead," Nietzsche writes, and we are all responsible for this murder. "God is dead," means that God died on the Cross 2000 years ago. And so let's not talk about it anymore. The consequence of this death of God: moral values are discordant, and all Western culture, of Christian obedience for 2000 years, is in crisis because nothing has replaced this culture, this Christian morality. It follows that the postmoderns no longer believe in God (one of the true meanings of "God is dead").

In these conditions of the disappearance of the culture stemming from ecclesial Christianity and the disappearance of belief in the Christian God, what becomes of man? Through his research, Michel Foucault observes that it is not so much the death of God that Nietzsche announces, but the death of man. It is consciously that the last man, in *Thus Spoke Zarathustra*, killed God, and no one can wipe the blood from his knife: by emptying the sea of water, man has emptied man and finds himself alone. He must answer for his own finitude. Thus, Nietzsche announces the death of the murderer of God, that is to say the end of man in philosophy, in language, in literature. The episteme of the late 18th century was linked to the disappearance of Discourse. Even if language emerges in our difficult-to-think postmodernity, man is dead. In these conditions, should we give up on thinking about man? We will think about man in his difficulties. Despite everything, man is a recent invention, but his figures have disappeared.

It is hardly easy to determine man and his transhumanist forms in a history of postmodern humanity that experiences the absence of man. So, to think about everything in the void of the disappeared man is to try, despite everything, to establish the meaning of the posthuman. For example, what becomes of man in the "advancements" of techno-sciences, in the digital realm? The paradox of man, absent from our postmodernity and having to decide on his own human becoming, is indeed contradictory. This will have to be overcome. Here arises the question of the limits of the human, that is, of its artificial evolution through technology. It follows that the "advancements" of the digital realm lead us to think about man differently, that is, in man wounded by himself. Is this death of man confirmed by the industrial revolution? We can no longer think about man and his limits with the cyborg, with man amputated of his historical past, of his feelings, of his natural emotions…Yet are we still human when we participate in this operation of decerebration of the human with digital tools that are similar to children's toys.[92]

Let us consider the human and his limits as fundamental data, a harmful consequence of the death of man. Our digital postmodernity is based on the dual foundation of the death of God and the death of man. Techno-scientific "advancements" invite us to a redefinition of the human as posthuman. Does an end of man lead to an end of the human because of its dangerous inventions (atomic bomb, mechanisation, transhumanism, attacks of man against the planet such as pollution, depletion of the earth's resources…)?

In this case: "science without conscience is but the ruin of the soul." This formula from Rabelais, drawn from biblical proverbs, seems far from today's scientists. By expelling morality (the science of good) from science, it shows that science and scientists are self-sufficient and know everything about our world that they want to bring closer to us. But by expelling moral truth and moral considerations, they deprive man of the conscience of good and evil, of the good act and the bad act. Techno-sciences-digital present no moral and metaphysical concerns. Indeed, postmodern science has nothing to say about feelings, the meaning of existence, or the enigma of suffering.

---

[95] Michel Foucault: Les mots et les choses, Gallimard, 1988, Paris.

On this point, Husserl writes: *"Our humanity is abandoned to the upheavals of destiny."*

In this context of the death of man, we can no longer speak of anthropology or of the Anthropocene, that is to say etymologically in "the era of the human," where is the reasonable human in techno-scientific theses? The influence of humans on the planet turns into an ecological catastrophe, into the dissolution of the human in technology. On this point, Antoine Vidalin is right to write about digital existence as a negation of the flesh, since the person disappears under the blows of techno-sciences. Man, already disappeared, confirms his death in the relationships and transformations of his being by what remains of science.

The human being struggles to exist in the plural as a species, as a subject, as an intelligent being endowed with reason, but who has become unreasonable. This is the death of man. What has he done with his reason in the digital adventure, and more specifically in the smartphone adventure? Can man remain human in a technological world? Who enslaves him? What remains of the human being? And is it even a chance to be born human? (As if one could be born other than human.) Can one be born a cyborg, or does one become one? These are strange questions to link to the death of man and the death of God. For here, God has disappeared as much as man in the conquest of nature, the conquest of space, and in the "transhuman" will to make man a posthuman. The very idea of the posthuman is surprising and illogical, as if one should move on to something else (like transforming the human into a posthuman). It appears that the posthuman logically emerges from what makes him human: his culture, civilisation, sensitivity, specificity, emotions, and desire to be recognised.

4. "THE PROMETHEAN SHAME", A CONSEQUENCE OF THE HUMAN AND ITS LIMITS.

Very early, humans showed a desire to appropriate technology: in "Protagoras", Plato describes the myth of Epimetheus and Prometheus as a usurpation of technology by humans. How to explain this usurpation? In nature, man is weak. At the beginning of humanity, animals and humans were given qualities. Epimetheus gave speed without strength to some animals... And when it came to man, he had no qualities left to pass on. Man found himself fragile in nature. Prometheus (the one who thinks ahead) had the idea to steal from Hephaestus and Athena the knowledge of the arts with fire. From then on, "man thus had science to preserve his life", and fire is at the origin of all techniques.[93][94][95]

There are lessons to be learned from this theft of fire. First, Prometheus was punished by Hephaestus. He was to be chained to a rock, and an eagle would come every day to devour his liver, which would constantly grow back (Hercules would free him). Then, man became a slave to technology. The humanity of Prometheus and Epimetheus is not a serene humanity; there was violence due to an original destitution, a weakness of man. Also, this violence allowed man to occupy a good place by defying the gods. This myth shows that man humanised nature by force, that is, he imposed the technical blade of fire on it. This has the consequence of exiting the initial human condition. This human will to defy the gods opens the way not to a limit, but to excess for man who is supposedly finite and limited. By exceeding the limits assigned to him by nature, man begins his Anthropocene poorly. Investing nature with techniques is, first and foremost, to rise above animals and exercise one's own freedom.

Other examples show the human will to transgress the laws of God. Adam and Eve disobeyed God: they tasted the forbidden fruit, that is, the fruit of knowledge. This is why God punished them by casting them out of Paradise and condemning them to suffer, to earn their living by the sweat of their brow. Adam and Eve ignored the limits set by God. This myth of original sin raises the problem of obedience and transgression of the forbidden. We find this will for independence, for the exercise of one's own freedom in today's issues of research on man and technology.

Going beyond measure is often a constant in man, and we will not be surprised by research on embryos, on digital technology, on techno-sciences. The biggest problem today is the lack of conscience, of ethics in the voluntary modifications of man on man and for man in his confrontation

[96] Edmund Husserl: La crise des sciences européennes et la phénoménologie transcendantale, Gallimard, 2019, Paris.

[97] Antoine Vidalin: Personne! L'existence numérique ou la négation de la chai, Artège, 2021, Paris.

[98] Plato, Protagoras: 320c-322d.

with techno-sciences. Unknowingly, the postmodern takes the place of God by modifying man and creation. In this state of bad spirit, Günter Anders gives the name "Promethean shame", that is

"The shame that seizes a man in front of the humiliating quality of the things he himself has made."[96]

Shame is a deliberate act (being ashamed of oneself), therefore a relationship with oneself, but one that fails. It should be a disturbance of oneself. But this Promethean shame is hardly felt by transhumanist researchers. The modifications on man by man lead us to a humanity without shame and without freedom. What is striking in G. Anders' analyses is the status of freedom:

"The subject of freedom and that of submission are reversed: things are free."

It is man who is not."

Man should be ashamed of what he is, of having become a new hybrid species; that is, according to G. Anders, the shame of man in front of the machines he has created: "the machine that becomes more ingenious than the engineer."[97] Since 1956, Anders sees man's ability to manufacture robots that, in turn, manufacture other robots without any human intervention. Man gets rid of his own discernment and becomes a slave to his inventions.

Since Prometheus stole fire, technology has always assisted man, and in this sense, he moves away from nature. It is known that for Descartes, in his "Discourse on the Method," man must *become master and possessor of nature*; that is to say, he must invest in nature to domesticate it, modify it so that he is no longer afraid of immensities. By defying nature, humans have no limits. On this point, Francis Bacon, one of the pioneers of scientific thought in the 16th century, considers technology as a power of increasing human power. He wants nature to be observed through inductive reasoning. Therefore, humans no longer want to be slaves to nature.[98]

---

[99] Günter Anders: L'obsolescence de l'homme. Sur l'âme à l'époque de la deuxième révolution industrielle (1956), Ivréa éditions, 2008, p. 37, Paris.

[100] Ibid., p.50

[101] Ibid., p.50

5. DO TECHNO-SCIENCES GO BEYOND HUMAN LIMITS?

Techno-sciences (Gilbert Hottois's expression) refer to the heavy intertwining between techniques and sciences, often without consciousness and respect for humans. There is concern about the advances in techniques and sciences. The scientist observes reality less; he wants to invest it through technology. But this techno-science is reduced by Michel Puech to technology without wisdom. Even if this term techno-sciences is used by scientists, it is up to us to use it also in the conflicting relations between techno-sciences and ethics, between true humanism and transhumanism, between posthumanism and criticism of human limits, between ecological crises and industrial societies, between the nuclear threat and the unconscious human of his own deadly civilisation that he himself has caused. [99]

Is technology a blessing or a danger to humanity? This question falls within human limits. Indeed, the essential thing is to see the consequences of the application of technology. On one hand, for Marx, technology is specific to human beings in that it is the ability to act on nature. Unlike animals, incapable of representing their actions before carrying them out, only humans improve their techniques in that technology depends on a consciousness that starts making plans. On the other hand, technology for Heidegger is a means to certain ends; it is "the instrument", the manufacture of tools and machines, but these applications of technology bring about a new form of humanity, very different from antiquity and modern times: our postmodernity invites us to think of man as finite. Technology acts like a boomerang; it reflects back to man, to his (re)definition, to his place in the world. Promethean shame should constantly resurface in front of the things invented by man. In fact, technology has classified man: he goes from humanity to any object in the digital world. Therefore, the question of the obsolescence of man arises:

"If man is obsolete, it is because he has acquired the status of a commodity, and of all commodities, man is the most outdated."[100]105

---

[102] Since Descartes' injunction to control nature, humans have gone too far: they ravage and disorient nature through pollution of the seas and overexploitation of the earth's resources. Here again, humans have crossed the limits. They destroy nature through their technological advances.

[103] Here, we have seen Michel Puech's thesis on technology: Michel Puech: Homo sapiens technologicus, op. cit.

In 1956, Anders criticised television (technical instrument) as "the world delivered to your home." Today, social networks go much further: humans share their thoughts and their lives with other humans. All this without real discussion: our data is taken without our consent. As a result, social networks limit and compartmentalise humans in a morbid contemplation of screens and take the form of a digital pacifier, always far from the truth, feelings, and emotions: through anarchic connections, as we have seen, humans do not grow, they do not learn anything, they are even less educated.[101]

Indeed, nothing increases his knowledge because he is trained to remain confined to his achievements, and everything prevents him from thinking. He cannot digest the overflow of information available to him. He does not assimilate anything because he prefers to connect and disconnect: this smartphone connectionism takes the form of dehumanisation. Let us add, with Anders, that *"dehumanization does not frighten the dehumanized because it is not within his jurisdiction."*

Techno-sciences go far beyond human limits and put them in danger. That is to say, technology takes power over humans, especially in the question of robotic technology. The issue of this question was raised by H. Arendt in *"The Human Condition"*:

"Should man adapt to the machine, or should the machine adapt to the nature of man?"

Humans have invented robots to make their lives easier, but in reality, they are surpassed by them. For example, Gilbert Simondon, in *«Du mode d'existence des objets techniques»*, writes:

"Man then abdicates before the android machine [robot imitating humans with emotions...] and bequeaths it his humanity," that is, in his relationship

---

[104] The concept of technology, from the Greek "tekhnè," refers to material production or fabrication. Technology is often confused with industry. Even though the Middle Ages considered technology as non-precious knowledge, with Descartes and Bacon, technology becomes a reality thanks to the notion of progress in humanity. Today, technology is part of our humanity because it relieves us of material concerns, but it drifts in its use to build a new man: the posthuman.

[105] G. Anders: L'obsolescence de l'homme, op. cit., 100

with the robot, man is no longer human in the sense of a thinking, speaking being, with a history, with states of mind, wanting to learn, progress, live with other humans in reasonable dialogue. The robot is a product of imagination, and man has transmitted his humanity to it as if he wanted to get rid of it as a burden. This transfer of humanity is surprising. For example, a statue is the product of the artist's imagination. But the robot is not human and it performs tasks programmed by man. It is a crude imitation of the human. So, an unhealthy competition plays out between the human and the robot, and the human part is won by the robot. This is where the absurdity of unbridled, uncontrollable technology comes into play, questioning our humanity. And so, technology is humanised, and man is dehumanised, or rather, he becomes a poorly refined object that does not expect a sculptor. It is man who adapts to the machine and becomes its slave in this posthuman or, more precisely, post-inhuman era. As a result, man has moved away from his human condition, wrote H. Arendt in 1958. He no longer admires nature. Humans are no longer children of nature but children of techno-sciences. This is explained by human desire to transform into a hybrid that wants to find a place not on earth but in the universe. Indeed, man has moved from nature to technology and finally to the conquest of the moon and "our planetary system." Because man has nothing more to learn from the earth, he turns his gaze to space. (Man is in the technical world while animals are still in nature).[102]

It is known that this technical adventure has always ended badly. For example, in the myth of Icarus, no lessons were learned from "hubris," this excess (the opposite is).[103]

"sophrosunê": moderation, prudence, wisdom).108 Indeed, let us not be like Icarus who burned his wings wanting to defy the Cosmos. The consequence of this myth: Icarus went too far ("hubris") and he was punished by the gods. This story also shows that the technique is poorly mastered. Humans need technical assistance even though they are destined to walk on earth and not to climb into the skies and lead an artificial life. He has always been encouraged to go beyond the earth. This often ended badly, as in the explosion of the Challenger shuttle in 1986. We can deduce that the Greeks

---

[106]   G. Anders: L'obsolescence de l'homme, op. cit.

[107]   Robot, a word of Slavic origin: "robota", which means work, from robotavat: to work.

knew that humans must not go beyond the limits of the earth: the conquest of space by techno-sciences causes us to abandon the earth and seek to settle elsewhere as if humans were unhappy with their condition and their mastery of nature. Now his plan is to conquer the other planets (to settle there and exploit the resources) and undoubtedly to destroy them.

We know that Icarus lived in Crete as a child. His father, Daedalus, an engineer, architect, created a maze for King Minos in order to enclose Minos' son. The minotaur, half-beast, half human, had been bewitched by Poseidon (god of the sea). Ariadne, daughter of Minos, did not want Icarus to get lost in the maze. So Daedalus, seeing the birds, had the idea of collecting their fallen feathers and adding wax, he stuck them on his arms and those of his son. Then they flew away. But Icarus flew too close to the sun and the wax melted: he fell into the sea and got drowned.

Techno-sciences lead humans to surpass limits, to create a new world, a techno-digital world, to conquer other planets. Be careful: by constantly looking at the skies, make sure not to fall into a well like Thales. Humans must remain in their dialoguing humanity and, therefore, use reason to behave properly.

6. EXAMPLE OF MANIPULATION OF HUMAN INTELLIGENCE BY ARTIFICIAL INTELLIGENCE.

In 1950, Alan Turing, a British mathematician, is a pioneer of "thinking" machines.

Taking the form of a discussion with the human[109], with ChatGPT released in November 2022, we are in a parody of knowledge and intelligence: you can ask to write a dissertation (poor), a cooking recipe, an imaginary dialogue (...), all at the same time. The work is done by an artificial intelligence (AI) which provides you with new content (videos, images, texts, news, instant translations, consultation with virtual psychologists, psychoanalysts...) based on data. The GPT chat gives the illusion of a machine that reasons, that thinks for us, and therefore we no longer need to think. Man no longer seems to control his own understanding: he is controlled by the machine, he becomes its slave because it guides him, influences him, dictates what he should think. He no longer practices maieutics (Socratic method).

This resignation of human intelligence in the face of artificial intelligence is bewildering. The famous ChatGPT is not situated between myth and technological revolution, but between the end of man and freedom of thought. The drifts in its use and its inability to truly think cause indigestion of knowledge, questions, and dubious answers to infinity. This chat GPT uses Artificial Intelligence (AI) as a conversational relationship with knowledge production. It answers questions in our place. And what are we good for? We now have AI as the pinnacle of illusory anthropology since we have the impression of talking to a human. And again, as we have seen with Plato, we must unmask the illusion in front of this techno-digital innovation.

Once again, this is about the use we make of this ChatGPT, especially in the endless data of knowledge based on our questions. Beware of human manipulation by AI. In reality, one can consider that ChatGPT is a revolution of intelligence and knowledge, but a manipulated knowledge, often thoughtless and distorting human intelligence. By talking to this AI, we forget that it is hardly an authentic human, and this illusion is not always unmasked. On the contrary, humans are subjected to the responses and knowledge of AI. The discussion of man with an inhuman, a technical object becomes a new non-philosophical language because only man possesses speech and intelligence: a disembodied entity like ChatGPT cannot replace man and his reason.

In the case of students, what havoc it causes, especially in their relationship to the knowledge they are supposed to learn and discern! They are, above all, consumers of knowledge in the exercise of intelligence. This work is given to AI. Learners can ask questions to AI, which would encourage them to no longer discover anything and learn by themselves. Producing a ready-made dissertation by this AI is nothing more than refusing to think for oneself and therefore letting the AI, this artificial box, think for you. In this case, students would no longer educate themselves and learn absolutely nothing. Furthermore, this AI does not teach honesty, human relationships, peace among men, fraternity, or how to help those who have fallen in this existence.[104]

It follows that a competition between AI and human intelligence is engaged, as if this scrap metal box, having followed no learning, could provide indications on life, justice, happiness... For example, comparing a philosophy dissertation written by AI would be a devaluation of our humanity. Because it is no longer the human leading the world, but the

"gadgets" invented by him. And what about purely human intelligence? Especially since today, we already lead a passive life, disconnected from pure humanity.

With ChatGPT, we find ourselves in impure humanity and a questioning of the status of school, learning the basics, and studies in general. The purpose of schools and universities is to educate and awaken the intelligence of students, yet with the advent of AI, this work is left to the care of this inhuman robot. What about the young person, the student, and their moral, intellectual, and philosophical education? AI is a virtual tool that thinks too quickly and arrogantly thinks in our place. The human comes first; it is up to him to control the digital techniques he has invented. It is too easy to leave this freedom to the techno-digital: let us overcome our temptation to resign, to stop reasoning in front of AI.

Finally, we hardly see how artificial intelligence would be a continuation of philosophy by other means. This statement, which parodies Von Clausewitz's formula (war is the continuation of foreign policy by other means), confuses human intelligence and artificial intelligence. It is another way of equating the two intelligences. However, natural intelligence and artificial intelligence have a close relationship with,

"Abstract principles of mental organisation," therefore, "legitimate distinctions between AI, psychology, and philosophy of mind seem to blend. And this unity would be called cognitive science. Certainly, there may be some conjunction, but it is better to consult the human psychologist than the artificial psychologist of AI. It follows that AI is often used (when taking a

[109]   La Croix du 29-04-2023, Paris.

Alexei Grinbaum: Alexei Grinbaum: Paroles de Machines (Humensciences), 1923, Paris, p. 192

plane...) but the Socratic-type debate, the search for problem resolution among humans hardly needs AI: peace, justice, happiness, morality are concepts experienced and discussed by humans. AI hardly has this experience. And there is a danger in trusting, admiring AI: human intelligence is unique. It is not because he has hands that man is intelligent but because man is intelligent that he has hands, as explained by Aristotle. Faced with AI, let us revalue human intelligence with this formula from Bergson:

"But what is intelligence? The way of thinking. It has been given to us, like the instinct of the bee, to guide our conduct."

7. THE ISSUES OF TRANSHUMANISM

Today, transhumanism, a frightening doctrine, wants to use science combined with techniques to transform man and his condition in order to move towards posthumanism. This transhumanist project alone shows that humans are dissatisfied with their limited, finite, mortal condition. Once again, there is a human desire to change their situation, to move from a purely human and mortal condition with its faults, joys, sorrows to a supposed immortal, eternal condition without suffering and difficulties of living. Illegal transhumanism favours reason (to be seen), progress (which ones?), and values (which ones?)[105]

Through the means of science and technology, transhumanism questions the human and its limits. For example, by delaying ageing and death, and by significantly developing intellectual and physical capacities. In this, transhumanism opposes the creation of man by God. However, we know from several passages of the Bible that humans are creatures of God, created from all eternity:[106]

"Before I formed you in the womb, I knew you." Jeremiah 1-5[107]

---

[110] Giovanni Landi: Intelligence artificielle comme philosophie, Les éditions Ovadia, 2022, pp. 122-123

[111] Henri Bergson: La pensée et le mouvant, P-U-F., 1992, Paris

[112] In 1957, Julian Huxley (brother to Aldous Huxley) may be the inventor of the concept of transhumanism. Transhumanism allows for the improvement of humans through genetic selection, known as eugenics. The prefix "trans" means transformation of the human species to perfection. The paths traced by transhumanists allow for posthumanist theses on a humanity devoid of biological meaning and replaced by technological innovations.

"For you created my inmost being; you knit me together in my mother's womb," Psalm 139:13.

"Thus says the Lord, your Redeemer, who formed you from the womb: I am the Lord who has made all things." Isaiah 44-24.

In our postmodern civilisation, the scientist, the futurist, the transhumanist, the AI fanatics (...), want to oust God: they claim to remake human creation according to their techno-scientific views. But do they have the same powers as the God of the Bible? This question seems incongruous, absurd in the eyes of God, being infinite, unlimited and man, being finite, limited, "incapable of all knowledge," "foolish worm" as Pascal writes in his

"Thoughts". Futurists, transhumanists, scientists, and managers of the GAFAM have expelled God to take his place and claim to create a new, artificial man, therefore emerging from laboratories, techniques...

It is, therefore, a question of thwarting God's creations to replace them with outrageous, even crude modifications of humans on humans. In this case, we completely depart from our initial human condition to enter a condition dictated by techno-sciences. Some, like Max More, are happy with this human deviation:

"We support the use of science to accelerate our transition from a human condition to a transhuman or posthuman condition."[108]

Transhumanism is indeed a posthumanism, that is to say, transhumanists demand to turn the page of humanity's history from the beginning to today. The future seems to be decided and therefore written in advance by humans. It is a terrifying future because it is inhuman, isn't it? Will man make way for posthumans, resulting from the crossing of biotechnologies, nanotechnologies, and artificial intelligence? Transhumanism is a posthumanism, that is to say, a dehumanisation of man. Man is no longer what he is when he becomes an improvised assembly, a mixture of machine and flesh, of natural intelligence and artificial intelligence.

On this point, the classic definition of man as a free being who decides his actions, who thinks for himself, who wants to discuss with others without intermediaries (cell phone...) is questioned with the still distant advent of a

---

[113]   Max More: Principes extropiens, 2002, Paris.

hybrid being. What becomes of the spirituality of man modified by techno-sciences? For the Greeks, man is a body and a soul; for transhumanism, man is a body and metal parts. Man is not willing to be a scrap heap that is thrown away when its parts are worn out. Nevertheless, it appears that it is the progress of the body and not of the mind that transhumanism proposes: it does not develop compassion, charity, peace, fraternal relations, morality, goodness, altruism...

The third industrial revolution (after the steam engine, oil, and electricity) is leading us into an artificial world in absolute discord with everything. There was something that existed and that made us still the heirs of humans. Posthumanism and transhumanism raise more than one question: 1. Does humanity have a future? 2. Will humans still be fully human? 3. Is transhumanism the end of man? 4. Is man playing God? 5. Does transhumanism illustrate the myth of eternity, of immortality? 6. Can the myth of eternal youth be achieved through transhumanism? 7. Does transhumanism raise the question of bio-medical ethics? Does transhumanism lead to a dehumanised posthumanism?

Any desire to go beyond the limits of human condition is decided by those who demand to embark on the uncomfortable adventure of transhumanism. Thanks to Kafka in "The Metamorphosis," we know that any change in human appearance poses a problem in relation to other humans. Indeed, Kafka depicts the modern world of work as alienation. For example, Gregor Samsa (a merchant), after sleeping, wakes up to go to work but realises that during the night, he has metamorphosed into a "monstrous insect," and even as an insect, Samsa is still within humanity. His loved ones reject him, but he remains human with his feelings and emotions: he retains empathy, even if his parents no longer look at him. It can be concluded that he remains human behind his animal appearance.

This brings us to the question: do we remain human in transhumanism? Having an insect head while still being fully human contradicts the transhumanist figure without human feelings or, more precisely, memories. Feelings are artificially modified. We are born human and become transhuman by losing the fullness of our humanity. Indeed, when we attack thought, emotions, and feelings, we attack rational freedom, the ability to choose between good and evil, to perform good deeds, and thus we question our original humanity.

With transhumanism, the aim is to deeply transform our human species and not simply undergo a metamorphosis in appearances, as in the example of Gregor Samsa. Transhumanists want to modify our being and control our thoughts by creating a new man, a cyborg, a mix of technology and human. In this case, let's talk about techno-human. If the goal is to allow humans to change sick or amputated organs, transhumanism can be accepted. But as soon as we touch thought, speech, or a modification of our being, the philosopher must reject this entirely invented and chimerical hybrid humanity. Is this still humanity? Is man still human? We have just outlined humanity and its limits: we do not touch the brain, as this would amount to mental manipulation carried out by gurus as in cults. This is why transhumanism is the cult of some scientists who want to bypass bio-medical ethics.

Certainly, as Georges Canguilhem writes in his article "Machine and Organism," mechanics must be inscribed in the organic. This means that we must understand that technical invention is "an effort by which man extends that of his organic existence." But this is hardly the question in the mutations proposed by transhumanism. It is about the claim to create a new man, that is, a posthuman. Therefore, posthumanism clearly states that we have turned the page on the human or that we are going to witness the extinction of the human species as it emerged from the hands of nature. Our humanity, in its transhumanist and posthumanist research, dissolves into the paganism of our postmodernity.

And G. Ganguilheim indirectly gives us the keys to understanding the harmful effects of transhumanism through his conception of technology:

"It is the rationalisation of techniques that makes us forget the irrational origin of machines, and it seems that in this field, as in any other, we must know how to face the irrational, even and especially when we want to defend rationalism." [115]

Is transhumanism a suspect rationalism when the classic man gives way to a hybrid being or a cyborg? The falsification of man in the innovation of the cyborg leads us to change civilisation, or rather, it is the end of man, the death of man. In transhumanism, reason, the ability to think and speak, dissolves. Indeed, in this anti-human adventure of transhumanism, transhumanists and futurologists want man to stop thinking for himself and to forcibly conform to a mould, to a pre-fabricated thought by all those who dream of an eternal, immortal human – an absurd thesis as it goes beyond the limits of the human. In reality, transhumanists hardly accept our free world: for them, freedom must be controlled and therefore no longer thought of in Greek categories. In other words, man must no longer be free to decide his actions. It follows that these fanciful theses, such as reversing death and improving our intellectual capacities, are obstacles to our humanity already wounded by the exactions of man (wars, difficulties of existence).

With Markus Gabriel, we have seen that the desire of some scientists to upload their brain onto an electronic chip in order to claim eternity is a fantasy, an absurd reasoning as if thoughts could be transmitted. This is where the excesses and dangers of the pseudo-scientific theses of transhumanism lie. Intelligence cannot be uploaded. By exalting so-called artificial intelligences, they have implicitly opposed them to human intelligences: humans already have difficulties in using their intelligence. Thus, scientists have introduced an illegal and improper competition between natural intelligence (reason) and artificial intelligence. Consequently, by glorifying technical or artificial intelligence, we go beyond the limits of the human. On this point, artificial intelligence will never be identical to true human thought according to Markus Gabriel. Let us prefer the model to the shapeless copy. Let us write with Koenig that artificial intelligence does not think, does not suffer, and does not love. Indeed, where are the human and moral feelings of artificial intelligence?

In our postmodernity, humans think less, or they allow themselves to be controlled by technical objects like smartphones and are seduced by the ideal of life proposed by excessive transhumanism. The problem of humans today lies in their refusal to think for themselves: they prefer to think through the suspicious applications of their smartphones. Therefore, they are already "guided" to think through artificial intelligence, a negation of the body and mind. Our humanity is delivered to algorithms that determine our destiny and our human history. Smartphone indigestion only increases with the multiple and unnecessary connections offered to internet users. This is a bad consequence of the death of man.

Are we going to let transhumanists and artificial intelligences, smartphone screens dictate our conduct, our morality, our being, our existence? It is normal to belong to the classic human species. Indeed, to be human in its fullness is first to reject the sharp modifications made to man by the double fanciful adventure of transhumanism and posthumanism, and then to accept reasonable dialogue, live in community, educate oneself, learn through every reading, every encounter, accept suffering as part of life, build happiness among other humans. In short, accept human relationships and not relationships with technology because man is not a disposable machine: he has feelings, emotions, and is called to be happy and to go through existence with its difficulties. Belonging to the human species is never a given once and for all; it is a belonging to a "praxis," that is, to a morality. Where is the moral dimension in the smartphone digital adventure?[109]

And the example of Covid-19 showed the racialisation of humanity, that is to say that the entire human species was not eligible for vaccines. The WHO called this "vaccine apartheid". Likewise, in terms of transhumanism, can we agree to separate the human species into the original human species and the technicalised human species? Will those who suffer the harmful attacks of transhumanism always remain fully human, belonging to the original human species, or belonging to a hybrid (metalised) human species? In other words, is transhumanism, which must lead to posthumanism, the end of our humanity? And will those who reject these crude transformations taking the form of techno-scientific assistants be ostracised?[110] Will they suffer the mockery of those who accept being hybrids? Such a competition, already launched by posthumanism, shows a death of man, a certain end of our classic humanity. There are therefore no limits to the transhumanist human because it is outside the philosophical and moral field. The classic human sees the collapse of his world, of his humanity taken from the hands

[114] Gaspard Koenig: La fin de l'individu. Voyage au pays de l'intelligence artificielle, Le Point, 2019, Paris.

[115] Gabriel Markus: Pourquoi la pensée humaine est inégalable?
    Markus Gabriel: Pourquoi la pensée humaine est-elle inégalable? Éditions J.C. Lattès, 2019, Paris.

of nature. For example, the science fiction of "Planet of the Apes" by Pierre Boule clearly shows the destruction of the world of men to be replaced by a world of monkeys. And we see that the apes behave like men and who have taken power by living on the vestiges of the human past (certainly the nuclear bomb was used and the last survivors became the slaves of the apes). It could be that a variation of this scene plays out between man and man. Indeed, in transhumanism, there is a certain denaturation of the human, that is to say in the forced departure from nature. Man is made to live with and in nature. Transhumanism introduces disorder, a denaturation with technological advances. On this point, we know how much Vercors in "Animaux dénaturés" greatly regrets having introduced techniques into human culture. There is an indefiniteness, that is to say an absence of limit, of finitude between the human and the technique, between the human and its denaturation. To this, Jean-Michel Besnier gives the name of the sin of modernity, a sort of imposture that augmented man is the posthuman. 118

The illusion of the remodelled and self-fabricated man introduces us to the era of artifice and the natural, of technology and the human body, of the human and the robot. The body, my body, is modified; it is no longer myself but an artificial self, a product of posthumanism. Non-biological intelligence will make humans any object in their artificial world. A frightening future is brewing, as Professor Hiroshi Ishiguro, a specialist in android robots, says: "One day, robots will be able to fool us into believing that they are human."119 The human dream of building on our own forces: is another human possible in posthumanism? In any case, we would then witness a pure and simple disappearance of the human species which has been evolving for thousands of years. Man is the murderer of himself in the transhumanist adventure. In other words, posthumanism would put an end to our humanity and to humanity: man would no longer carry his cultural heritage, and words would no longer have meaning. Is this really reasonable? The cyborg or the bionic man replaces the moral man, the man of nature, the man of pure feeling120. In this case, we fall into the absurd, and the words no longer have a human meaning but a transhumanist meaning: humanism must not be replaced by posthumanism. This disembodied world, excessively falsified by artificial intelligence and techno-sciences, will choose the human and make it solely material. Where is the spiritual power of humans? It is very curious to claim to go towards the non-human! Nietzsche wrote that man is raw material, poorly roughed up, and he is waiting for someone to carve him. Is it transhumanism or posthumanism? Neither. Like Nietzsche, we must return to the glorification of the earth. Otherwise, we then move from anthropology to anthropotechnics or anthropotechnics taking the form of posthumanism. Certainly, it is hardly a question of becoming a minoseist, that is to say having the hatred of technology, because technology is an activity of man, the means to certain useful ends to help our humanity and not to deprive it of its essence to replace it with an artificial man or an unreasonable android robot.[116][117][118]

But in front of these android creations, theologian Charles Delhez reassures us: *"[These androids] can send emotional feedback and evoke empathy. Having identified the emotions, they respond to them with gestures, facial expressions that give the illusion that they are sensitive to them. But, truth be told, no matter how much of an android it is, the machine does not have a real face. It only mimics friendship. It only gives the illusion that it has become attached to us. It may have an external voice, but not an internal one."*

Therefore, delineating the boundaries of the human and its limits is to show the progress of technology (fraudulent terms). It is then a matter of defining man, or more precisely, redefining man. This implies first talking about his past, about humanisation; that is, the transition from nature to culture but also from animality to humanity. Let us add that man is first and foremost a product of nature. Today, we are faced with another transition and another definition of man: the transition from man of culture, of civilisation (through his way of life) to the posthuman, a human-technical being that could, as we have seen, be a deception; that is to say, the posthuman is no longer human in the classic and natural sense of the term. It is what the technology incorporated into his body has made of him; that is to say, a robot, an android, a competitor of natural and cultural man.

Let us refuse the future to be built and dictated by the power of GAFAM and by authoritarian regimes ready to control the global population, to manufacture children in laboratories according to their needs and the roles

---

[116]   Jean-Michel Besnier: Demain les posthumains, édition Pluriel, 2017, Paris.

[117]   Ibid. p.119

[118]   Georges Canguilhem: "machine et organisme", op. cit., p. 127.

they occupy in society. On this point, in "Brave New World," novelist Aldous Huxley (born 1932) shows the manipulation of consciences by political power where critical thinking is banned. So, let us not allow transhumanism to take place (inspired by cyberpunk: a culture from the 1980s convinced that our world has an apocalyptic future).

Let us add that transhumanist technologies go too far in modifying the human and its production. Indeed, transhumanist medicine claims to change the nature of man and animal (growing a human ear in an apple, giving birth to a piglet with a human heart, implanting human neurons in the brains of mice to make them smarter...). Doctors, with the complicity of engineers and computer scientists, play at being sorcerers by denaturing our humanity, by crossing it with animals... All for the utopia of eternal life. What will a society of elderly people remade by transhumanist medicine be like compared to the younger generations? It is considering humans as guinea pigs. Let us reject these experimental transformations of the human.[114]

121 Florence Pinaud, Elodie Perrotin: Qui sont les Trans humanistes? Éditions Ricochet, 2019. This is the conclusion of these two authors (p.105): *"When we talk about transhumanism, we often end up talking about the video game Deus Ex Human Revolution. In 2027 (of this game), man has often taken control of his evolution. But this control is essentially in the hands of the largest multinational corporations engaged in a fierce commercial war over bionic implants. Implants poorly tolerated by the body, which forces those who wear them to take an expensive drug to cope. The Deus scenario does not take sides for or against. In its universe, characters have the choice to be implanted with prostheses that turn them into war machines or not. And whether you play with or without implants, you have as many advantages as disadvantages. "Other video games depict the promises and pitfalls of transhumanist technologies. In Bioshock, the metropolis Rapture built at the bottom of the ocean is a city in decline. Controlled by science for decades, it has abused genetic modifications. Today, its inhabitants have become monsters addicted to a substance that gives more or less superpowers. The hero of the game himself is a genetically modified baby to become an adult very quickly. He discovers that he is Demiurge's son*

---

[119] Charles Delhez: Où allons-nous? De la Modernité au Transhumanisme, éditions Salvator Fidélité, 2018, p. 135, Paris

(the universal creator) who created this city with apocalyptic appearances and tries to regain its control.[115]

Transhumanism appears as a technico-religious sectarism. It does not respect our initial human condition as defined by nature. Let us be cautious while listening to the dialogue between transhumanists, philosophers, futurologists, journalists, doctors, nanotechnologists, biologists, cyberneticians, and representatives of GAFAM. And the human does not have to be replaced by beings of his own invention. It cannot be confused with creatures that are part machine, part-organism; it must distance itself from this fantasy of the posthuman.

8. DOES THE MACHINE (AI) HAVE THOUGHTS AND MORALS?

This question arises for a human, but not for machines made by humans because they have neither reason nor soul. Turning to the special issue of the philosophy magazine, we find relevant questions in line with our sick postmodernity. Are artificial intelligences our slaves, friends, or masters? Will an algorithm moralise us? Is a conscious and moral machine possible?

In our humanity, wounded by the distance from God, we already have difficulty establishing human relationships. So, what can be said about man in his relationship with techno-sciences? We have already seen that thinking consciousness and moral consciousness belong only to humans. But with the invention of machines (computers, AI, robots, androids...), where is the human? Where is true reason as the faculty of thinking and speaking, a privilege of man?

It is nonsense, a logical error to anthropomorphise artificial intelligence and other inventions in general. Techno-sciences are not anthropomorphic. They remain inventions without humanity. For example, a machine cannot have consciousness, morals, or freedom to act. Only a being of flesh and bone like man remains human when he exercises his freedom, when he thinks, when he acts with discernment. A machine does not invent religion and therefore does not invoke God (it does not practice forgiveness, charity...).

That a (moral) consciousness can be created in the printed circuits of artificial intelligence is pure fantasy and ignorance. Because there is no

[120]   Être humain? (Edited by Jean Birnbaum), Gallimard, 2022, p. 32, Paris

computer conscious of its actions, of what it does. Here, for man, the word consciousness means knowledge returning to itself, while the computer obeys the functions for which it has been programmed. To be a moral consciousness, one must first be a thinking consciousness, that is, reflective. But a machine does not perform acts of moral consciousness. AI does not belong to our humanity, but to technology and science. Indeed, AI is not human but inhuman. It does not exercise its freedom in the manner of a man. The Ten Commandments are made for humans and not for techno-sciences. The designers of AI machines claim, against all common sense, that

"We attribute things like motivations, intentions, and self-consciousness to our brain, which, in fact, is just a complex system without a unifying agent." [122]

But humans know how to unify, reason, make projections, and build their future. They are sensitive, fragile, ambitious, and charitable [...]; these qualities do not belong to machines, and only man unifies his thoughts because he has reasoning, logic, and common sense. And let us remember that the machine has no religion: this relationship between man and divinity belongs to humans, as well as existential questions. A religious morality does not exist in techno-sciences. Speaking of a spiritual machine as Ray Kurzweil does is a philosophical heresy, a scam of thought. Because spirituality, religious morality (open morality and closed morality) belong only to humans. Here it is not man who pushes the limits, but rather the techno-sciences that want to play God and control humanity, or the GAFAM want the techno-sciences to take the place of God with humans. [116]

To show further the distancing of humans from their inventions, it can be asserted with Hubert Dreyfus that an artificial intelligence without a (human) body is an illusion. Man is a body with a soul added. However, the machine is entirely artificial matter. The body is reserved for man. The machine is not a body but a tangle of stupid materials without a soul and natural thought. This equality between man and machine was introduced by futurologists, dubious scientists... The machine is subject to man, but now he becomes its slave. For example, he becomes one with his smartphone because <u>he is always on</u> screens. Today, we are being made to think by machines

[122] Philosophie magazine, hors-séries, IA, le mythe du XXIe siècle, printemps 2023, p. 9, Paris

and not by ourselves. Man remains with his body, but now he becomes a mixture of machine and body. The machine wants to become human in the transhumanist adventure. A transhuman being is a violation of the laws of God and man. Because only man thinks and speaks. Since the machine does not have autonomous human-style thought, it does not necessarily retain its past. Only man retains his history. The AI lacks its history, unless it goes to find its prehistory in the 80s cartoon, "Captain Future": Professor Simon Wright having died, his brain was transplanted into a mini robot (with a transparent dome) and continues "to think", to speak, to give advice: he is a walking brain without a body.

Similarly, Toshino, the designer of the Atlantis, the spaceship of Albator, the space corsair (80s cartoon), before dying, decides to implant his own brain into the computer that controls the Atlantis. So human intelligence and artificial intelligence become one, and Toshino continues to speak to Albator through the computer. This is a fiction taking the form of an inquiry into the reality of such an experience. Here can be found a practical history of techno-sciences in fiction. Should we be worried about it? Daniel Andler responds reassuringly in these terms:

"[...] It seems to me that we are still far from the 'ultimate' goal: that of creating intelligent machines. AIs know, quantitatively, how to do more and more things; but as Hubert Dreyfus nicely put it, it is not by climbing to the top of a tree that you get closer to the Moon. You are still far from being able to travel the space between the earth and its satellite, even by a few meters. To say that GPT-4, because it does increasingly amazing things, is approaching general artificial intelligence, and therefore human intelligence, is part of this illusion. The most insightful AI researchers acknowledge that current systems are still 'very stupid'. In my opinion, the 'still' is unnecessary."

On the difference between human intelligence and artificial intelligence, there is no superiority. It will never cease to be written that the media and business people, with the complicity of certain dubious engineers and scientists, have introduced this competition between man and machine. However, the machine is not as intelligent as man. And even if it is capable of falsifying information and images, it remains clearly inferior to human intelligence. For example, the whimsical Marvin Minsky, computer scientist and mathematician ("The Society of Mind," Dunod edition, 1980), invites to build a mind, that is to say an inevitably artificial soul. Such a claim is a lack of reflection and misanthropy. This scientist wants to play God with the same powers. But he forgets that a construction of a soul can be called artificial intelligence, that is to say a degraded intelligence, a "soul" mortal. Therefore, techno-sciences have become the new religion of scientists, technicians, and business people. This shows that man, faced with the machine, needs a certain sacredness. But is a pagan or profane sacredness still sacred?[117][118]

It follows that man presents a problem in front of the machine, taking the form of a lack of morality. In artificial intelligence, we witness a moral indifference or moral neutralisation to make room for "badness" and evil. Indeed, AI is amoral, and we cannot rely on it to make decisions, or it will make them wrong. In this regard, the animated series "Captain Future" from the 1970s already showed the absence of morality and therefore the harmful effects of computers because they have trivialised evil and immoral action. In fact, in one of the episodes, Captain Future is sent by the "intersidereal government" to a planet ruled by a despot. Towards the end of his investigation, he realises that the dictator, a computer endowed with intelligence and artificial language, terrorises the inhabitants. This episode, far from being useless, shows how the computer, designed by man or by robots, replicates the human pattern in its violence, domination, and glory. Ultimately, these machines behave very badly (like humans) even when they gain a certain autonomy from their creators: now the machines have the ability to make decisions and commit bad acts. The path of violence and therefore exaction is chosen by the computer. Such an option shows that moral consciousness does not exist in the computer.

From all this train of thought, let us reaffirm that moral consciousness is above all human: there is no moral machine, or else words have lost their meaning, and we find ourselves in nihilism—the end of man, the death of man. Even if man has difficulties in remaining moral, he is the only moral being to have the conscience of good and evil. The machine has the ability

---

[123] Hubert Dreyfus: What Computers Can't Do: The Limit of Artificial Intelligence (1972). This American philosopher (1929-2017) offers a critique of AI based on phenomenology theory. For him, computers can only deal with facts.

[124] Daniel Andler, Philosophie Magazine, hors-séries IA, le mythe du XXIe siècle

Daniel Andler: Intelligence artificielle, intelligence humaine: la double énigme, Gallimard, 2023, Paris.

to perform certain tasks, but it is unable to surpass man in his intelligence, in his existential questions, in his search for truth through and in public discussion. For example, ChatGPT is far from replacing humans in their feelings, emotions, hopes, and relationships with others. Humans hardly need to live with machines; they want to live with other humans. Aristotle's formula "every city is a community" cannot apply to machines. Human and machine are distinguished as sensitivity and inhuman neutrality.

9. Are goodness, God, and the sacred neutralised in transhumanism?

The postmodern is the newcomer of our world because, century after century, it wants to fulfil the dream of the past: to be all-powerful, infallible, immortal, creator of a new man through transhumanism. Paradoxically, to achieve this goal, man exceeds his limits by denying his humanity. He no longer wants to be fully human because it is a condition of suffering; he wants to escape suffering to be himself God. Hence the fanciful theories of Noah Harari in his book "Homo Deus" with this exclusive subtitle: "A Brief History of the Future." But this new world is not debated: the techno-sciences, the techno-digital impose their views without any serious debate. For them, digital and artificial science is their new certainty that they want to impose by force (of the GAFAM). The future is not debated but presented as a certainty. By what right can one attest to the future? Indeed, it is illogical to tell the story of the future. Speaking with certainty about the future, is it entering into illusion? And homo sapiens cannot become a "homo deus" as we have seen. Moreover, after sapiens, it is always up to sapiens to lead his world and to renounce becoming God. However, Harari shows, through his technicist vision of the world, that man is necessarily dominated by the digital, artificial intelligence... And that by becoming God, he will be happier. But what remains of humanity in a world entirely governed by the inhuman machine? We will suffer from having left our fully human world to enter a neo-pagan world where man will have nothing to do, nothing to say, but what remains of him, of his partial humanity, will be subjected to powerful technology. Where is the dignity of man within the limits of powerful technology?[119]

---

[125] Yuval Noah Harari: Homo deus, une brève histoire de l'avenir, Albin Michel, 2017, Paris.

As Rémi Brague points out, the idea of the dignity of man was based on a theological anthropology in philosophy. With transhumanism, anthropology has become a non-human digital technology and more deeply rooted in neo-paganism, in the absence of meaning of existence, in the forgetfulness of God. More precisely, we are in the era of "anthropotechnoscience", taking the form of an artificial intelligence that ruins our humanity. Is a human who is part man, part machine still human? A half human can only exist in the dangerous reveries of transhumanists. They mainly want to make humanity disappear from humans. As we have seen, we must think with the disappeared man. With the transhumanists, it is the illustration of the dissolution of man: they are misanthropes since they prefer the transhuman and for that, they need to commit the murder of man on man. Their alleged improvement of man through transhumanism is a techno-scientific delusion.

Transhumanism is beyond anthropology and theology. In reality, this doctrine opposes philosophy, morality, and all human categories. So, transhumanism and its twin brother posthumanism will make it impossible for humans to philosophise: they will have to rely on the digital to answer their existential questions when techno-sciences are incapable of doing so.

This old dream of man to dominate nature, but also God, is denounced by Rémi Brague in his book: "Le règne de l'homme.". Long before the foolish transhumanist project, there is already this desire to crown man, and especially to dethrone God and his creation. And man appears as a big upstart and usurper of authentic creation. This appropriation of the power to create is accompanied by an ignorance of the question of God, or more precisely, God no longer plays a part in the human project in transhumanism. Let's call this the indignity of man taking the form of a forgetting or a deliberate rejection of the sacred, a question that no longer arises in our time.

"techno-digital,"

So, it is a very ancient fact in the history of modernity to distance oneself from God and man. Our neo-pagan postmodernity only receives this anti-Christian heritage and this human desire to be the creator of himself. For example, Thoreau already complained that man was becoming "the tool of his tools.". This expression shows that man is his own toy. He is also the toy of political power that will not hesitate to monitor him, to level him, to colonise his intelligence. Man becomes "the toy of deceptive powers" embodied by the fantasies of futurologists...

To go further, the dream of the artificial or transhuman man is very ancient as Rémi Brague reminds us: Marc Shelley wrote his book "Frankenstein or the modern Prometheus" (1818). This story has had many variations and has distorted Shelley's novel. This human desire to create a man shows that Shelley, a neo-pagan, wants to have the same powers as God. In reality, the question of man-machine is part of Western history. Science wants an application of its principles to the world. The robot man is a very ancient vision that transhumanism tries to materialise through technology and digital. The world of tomorrow introduces us to a hybrid vision of man in total contradiction with nature and the creator God.[120][121][122]

The transhumanist adventure is carried out in an unavowed materialism and, therefore, in a project of a future without natural man and God. Before the development of the digital, we were already in neopaganism, the successor of ecclesial Christianity. Today, in these technological "advancements," we further reinforce this illegal neopaganism. We are neopagans because we have made the God of the Bible disappear, and even the futurologists, the transhumanists (...), have taken the place of God. The transhumanist adventure is solitary. And man (what remains of him through his own modifications) continues to look towards the cosmos without God. By his own digital decisions, the postmodern presents a desire to move away from his original human condition. This desacralised adventure is part of neopaganism. So man lives in a double amputation: he is amputated from himself and from God. That is why he is unwell, and our postmodern world suffers from this ailment. Because men take themselves for God and go too far, "further beyond."

Thus being, good, sacred, and God neutralise each other in the mad transhumanist adventure. This forgetting of the sacred causes the postmodern to live poorly. He lives in the profane, in what is outside of God, in neo-paganism. As humans are driven by "hubris" by technicised excess,

---

[126]   Rémi Brague: Le règne de l'homme, Gallimard, p. 246, Paris.

[127]   Julien Offray de la Mettrie: l'homme-machine, 1747, Paris.

[128]   Pascal Marin: le robot et la pensée, Cerf, 2019, Paris.

they refuse to ask themselves questions. Forgetting God is the rejection and abandonment of the Christian heritage.

10. The transhumanist project, an anthropophobia

The author "Pièces et main d'œuvre" (pseudonym) of the "Manifesto of the Future Chimpanzees" (against transhumanism) does us a great service by putting the right words on this transhumanist adventure, this foolish advent of a new man, a hybrid being, supposed to be superior in every way to the simple human being. The author warns us of experiments done on humans, on their emotions, intellect, and thoughts (reduction of thought activity by the suppression of free will...). Through techno-medicine and digital techno-science, the goal is to make disappear what man is by nature, that is to say, by birth, a being wanted and created by God.[123][124]

Human power is transferred to machines. We live in a "Smart City" that is nothing but a smartphone monitoring all our actions and "thoughts". Our lives would be led by computers. For example, Google wants to connect the smartphone directly to our brain so that we have infinite data, but which will hardly allow us to freely exercise our intelligence. In reality, we are already led by artificial intelligences. It is no longer a question of following the words of cybernetics founder Norbert Wiener, as reported by[125]

"Pièces et main d'œuvres": *"We have so radically modified our environment that we must modify ourselves to live on the scale of this new environment."*.[126]

Transhumanism is an extreme and inhuman programme that awaits us. It operates exactly on the notion of eliminating the weak, that is, those who refuse to be modified, to be enhanced by techno-sciences. Those are the chimpanzees of the future, that is, those who want to remain fully human because they love our humanity as it was intended by the creator. So, they

---

[129] Jacques Arnould: Quand les hommes se prennent pour Dieu, Salvator, 2020, p. 107, Paris.

[130] We know that Pierre Teilhard de Chardin wrote: "nothing but the earth is insufficient." (Lettres de voyage... Septembre 1926, Grasset, 1956, p.97). He was aware that man no longer looks at nature but at space. But Teilhard de Chardin's vision remains Christian, which is hardly the case for the neo-pagan transhumanists of our postmodernity.

[131] Cardinal Robert Sarah: Il nous a tant donné. Hommage à Benoît XVI, Fayard, 2023, Paris.

[132] Benedict XVI: Ce qu'est le christianisme, Éditions du Rocher, 2023, Paris.

remain faithful to God in a neo-pagan world, without morals, without real human values.[127]

With transhumanism, we enter into an anthropophobia, and the anthropophobes are preparing for the total destruction of our humanity. Hybridisation is already a rejection of the other man.

Far from being a philanthropy, we know that the transhumanist project is a visceral misanthropy, with the selection of human beings through eugenics and techno-science. Some will be half human and half robot, others will remain fully human.

Transhumanism is the opposite of humanism towards the other man. Because the other is excluded. Indeed, the other is always the poor, the one who has fallen in this life and who awaits a helping hand to lift him up. We know that the entire philosophy of Emmanuel Lévinas revolves around the relationship between me and the other, which is unconditional: the other is more important than me, one of the great principles of the Bible. Or, with transhumanism, there is a radical forgetting of the other man, an absence of humanism, of altruism. It could even be said that transhumanism is a radical misanthropy because transhumanists want to disfigure the original man and ultimately contribute to the physical disappearance of the human being. So we are in a death of man, of his spirit and his body. Only the void will remain, that is to say, extreme nihilism (words have no meaning).

Transhumanism, an anti-humanism, is a kind of artificialisation of the world without the support of the Good and the free subject. Beware of the manipulation of object men or machine men. We then witness a collective defeat of human thought if we accept to enter the transhumanist game. Under the guise of good intentions, of improving humanity, transhumanism goes beyond the good of the human. "Automachination or the manufacture of the man-machine" is the greatest catastrophe that our humanity could experience. Indeed, a human whose intellectual and physical capacity are enhanced by transhumanist work will move away from his humanity to enter an altered, even non-existent humanity. The techno-scientific ideology is leading our humanity astray because of a few who fascinate with their machine, with the complicity of the GAFAM: artificial intelligence,

---

[133] Pièces et main d'œuvres: Manifeste des Chimpanzés du futur, contre le transhumanisme, éditions Service compris, 2017, p. 75, Paris

nanotechnology... And extremism in the game of sorcerer's apprentices is found exactly in the following words:

"In April 2017, Facebook announced the study of a man-machine interface capable of transcribing the words thought by a human onto a computer to speed up text typing. With his new company Neuralink, Elon Musk, the transhumanist CEO of Tesla and SpaceX, wants to connect neurons to interfaces implanted in the brain. It is about creating a 'digital tertiary layer' above the limbic system and the cortex. Moving from the low-speed Cyborg, with its external prostheses (smartphone), to the high-speed Cyborg." [128]

In this context, an operation aiming to modify the brain seems like a crime against man and against God. Do we necessarily need a machine that directly transcribes our thoughts onto a smartphone? Is this not a violation of human rights and a very clever mental manipulation? We are in a dictatorship of the transhumanist mind that we find hard to digest, that is, to understand. Therefore, our future life will be smartphone-centric, a mix of smartphone and human. This results in a smartphone-human or a human-smartphone, no longer having true hope, as is already the case today with life unfolding on smartphone screens and the forgetting of people; it is a pre-negation of the flesh. This is a propaedeutic to transhumanism and posthumanism.[129]

Now, let's talk about the transhumanist as a proud being, a Promethean, meaning that he owes everything to himself and not to God and others. The transhumanist scientist carries within him the Promethean pride taking the form of a fairground buffoon. To this attitude of being the maker of his own machines and therefore an innovative Promethean, Günter Anders gives the name "self-made man", meaning that postmoderns desire to be manufactured and not born. Why does the Promethean want to manufacture himself according to G. Anders?

"If he wants to make himself, it is not because he can no longer bear anything that has been made, but because he refuses to be something that has

---

[134] Emmanuel Lévinas, L'humanisme de l'autre homme, Le Livre de poche (Biblio Essais), 1987, Paris.

[135] Manifeste des chimpanzés du futur, op. cit., p. 104

not been made; it is not because he is indignant at having been made by others (God, deities, nature), but because he has not been made at all and that, not having been made, he is therefore inferior to his products."139

Let us reaffirm that the distress of our humanity lies in this Promethean desire for make-up, self-reification: in transhumanism, man becomes a thing; he is an object that is part of a techno-scientific device. Is this truly the future of humanity?

11. IS TRANSHUMANISM THE FULFILMENT OF NIETZSCHE'S OVERMAN?

Many fantasists have believed to see in the overman the realisation of transhumanist theses. While there is indeed a fraudulent attempt here to appropriate Nietzsche's philosophy to justify the doctrine of transhumanism. First, what does the overman consist of?

In "Thus Spoke Zarathustra", under the chapter of "the higher man", Nietzsche evokes the figure of the overman. As "God is dead", everything is permitted, meaning that we can live without God and thus opens the possibility of the arrival of a superior man, the overman. In reality, the overman radically opposes the spirit of Christianity, since the two hardly teach the same doctrines.

Indeed, "Thus Spoke Zarathustra" is a dysangel. Nietzsche parodies the Gospels by reversing the values: to the idea of loving one's neighbour, Nietzsche opposes loving one's distant. The overman is not compassionate (compassion, according to Nietzsche, was considered a weakness among the Greeks). He does not want any pity, and he reproaches ecclesial Christianity for its doctrine of compassion for all, including, as Nietzsche says, "the weak" and the "failures". Now, the overman does not care for the poor, the widow, or the orphan. It should also be noted that he is part of radical neo-paganism. This neo-pagan era opens with the death of God that we have seen.

With the overman and the decline of moral values, we are no longer in humanity. We are in the forgetfulness of the classical man. Therefore, the human opposes the overhuman, as through these words of Nietzsche:

"Man is a rope stretched between the beast and the overman", or to put it another way:

"My brothers, what I can love in man is that he is a passage, a decline."

Nietzsche considers that man is corrupted by ecclesial Christianity and that his nature is deeply contradicted by the Christian doctrine, especially by its prohibitions. That is why Nietzsche invites us to turn towards the overman because he affirms life even though he is not a saint or a genius. Four senses of the overman can be seen: - that by which man can and must be overcome, - the overman is an individual, a superior man who transmutes all values, - one must be careful not to confuse the overman with evolutionism (cf. 341 of Nietzsche's "Gay Science"), - the overman is understood with the concept of eternal return of the same; it is a metaphor that designates a cyclical and repetitive time. The eternal return holds in the following idea: this life as you live it, do you want to live it again and eternally (and this spider returns and this plant, and this moonlight)? *Everything advances and everything returns, eternally rolls the road of existence.*[130][131]

Through these theses on the overman, one hardly sees an illustration of the absurd theory of transhumanism or posthumanism. Man is neither beast nor overman. He is poorly refined and awaits a sculptor. But he hardly awaits a transhumanist and dubious sculptor. For Nietzsche, man is a term, and the overman will succeed him. He is hardly a technico-digital being, nor a robot, nor an android, nor a cyborg. And this overman is entirely opposed to the philosophy of Christianity. Nietzsche rejects Christians because they are beings with moral precepts. Man is indeed an end. He will be replaced by a new type of man, richer in higher values, that is to say values of selfishness, inequality among men, rights for a few (the noble) who reject the "pessimism of weakness" according to Nietzsche.

Transhumanists are mistaken when they believe they can detect in Nietzsche's words the project of achieving the overman with the help of techno-sciences and thus improving the human. There can be no question

---

[136] Gunther Anders: L'obsolescence de l'homme, op. cit., vol. 1, p. 40

In the "self-made" concept, the self-posing ego of Fichte is found, that is to say, of the postmodern man who wants to be made by himself instead of being born. This has a rather moral and political sense. But it can be applied to the scientists of our time.

[137] Nietzsche, «Ainsi parlait Zarathoustra,» volume VI, p. 308.

of technology to achieve the realisation of the overman. The overman remains human with his biological body, and the transhuman is an artificial construction, as in the image of the improper cyborg.

Nietzsche uses the concept of the overman to reinforce his endless controversy against the ideals of ecclesial Christianity. In our theses on the achievements of the supposed death of man (this present work is volume III), we have mentioned man and his end following the death of God. And we can link transhumanism, and even more so posthumanism, to the end of Christian culture. Recall that the postmodern wants to think of life in non-Christian terms and wishes to move on to another culture: we have seen that transhumanism carries the doctrine of neo-paganism and therefore the end of compassion, respect for life, and the law of charity according to Saint Paul. In transhumanism, man has usurped the place of God. Therefore, he can only sink into materialism, selfishness, the crushing of the weak, and inequality among men... In this sense, transhumanism has links with Nietzsche's overman. In other words, these links are not found in technology or in improving the living conditions of men (pseudo-eternity, utopian disappearance of diseases...) but in anti-compassion, anti-ecclesial Christianity, and anti-fraternity. Therefore, transhumanism, "realising" the overman, is hardly an achievement of the death of man, but a step towards the nothingness of existence.[132]

In short, Nietzsche never showed any intention of creating a cyborg, changing human nature, or producing a hybrid being in a laboratory. He explains this clearly in "Ecce Homo".[133]

"To improve Man[...] that is the last thing I would ever think of promising. Do not expect me to erect any new idol. Let the old ones learn what it costs to have feet of clay."

"It is not enough to change the world. We change it anyway. It changes considerably even without our intervention. We must also interpret this change in order to change it in return, so that the world does not continue to change without us, and that we do not end up in a world without men."

---

[138]   Ibid.

[139]   Nietzsche: Ecce Homo, Preface, paragraph 2.

Günther Anders: L'obsolescence de l'homme, Volume II, sur la destruction de la vie à l'époque de la troisième révolution industrielle

Éditions FARIO, 2011, p. 7, Paris

Conclusion: Life Does Not Oscillate Between Connections and Disconnections

Scientists, futurologists, journalists, businessmen, GAFAM are shameless and immoral neoprometheans, unconcerned about humans and their well-being: they have put away God and his creation to become the new gods. Let us not be in smartphone iconomania, that is, the domination of images to infinity. "Smartphonism" has become the new religion of the postmodern. This doctrine consists of techno-sciences, artificial intelligence, the hope of becoming transhuman, that is, a hybrid being, half human, half metallic. Connectionism is not the faithful relationship between me and the other; it is not a meeting between an "I" and a "you", but a voluntary confinement leading us to the end of man. The digital has catapulted man into a carceral finitude where the past no longer matters, and the categories of freedom, morality, and reflection disappear. It is smartphone nihilism.

Our postmodernity, in rebellion against ecclesial Christianity, has lost its traditions. We know, with Hannah Arendt, that the current crises come from a serious problem relating to our relationship with tradition. The past is rejected, and our contemporaries look to the future with the hope of a world without disease, without old age, without death. The utopia of transhumanism comforts them in their choice to trust the invasion of GAFAM, as if it is a sign that life will be easier. But also, they forget that a worrying, suspicious world is emerging and overwhelming us with intentions, with confidence in technological innovations. However, this digital smartphone world has a criminal impact on the brains of young people. These people, always glued to the screens, do not know how to put their cell phones away, nor how to digest them, that is to say, how to control them: it is not up to the cell phones to control me, to master my life, but up to me to exercise absolute power over him. However, the smartphone has colonised our postmoderns and has become essential. Smartphone users who live in a continuous present, becoming one with their cell phones, radically forget the human past which built them and of which they are heirs whether they like it or not. With the emergence of digital and technical-digital life, the human past and tradition are forgotten, rejected as if they did not exist. And we suffer from this forgetting because we believe that the postmodern world begins with you and ends with you.

In 1956, Gunther Anders had already seen this distrust for the past of a nation, a culture, a civilisation. This is why he calls for building *"Molussia, a country whose past is full of lessons for the future."144*. A Molussian thought must be built because we are always heirs to a tradition that has bequeathed us its culture and its lessons. However, the human past, the history of humanity, is of little interest to transhumanists, GAFAMs, futurologists, smartphonists, and fans of uncontrolled digital technology.[134]

"A humanity that treats the world as a world worth throwing away, treats itself as a humanity good to throw away," 145 explains G. Anders. A disposable humanity is being built in the techno-scientific adventure. Our smartphone, digital, techno-scientific life has made direct relationships between humans disappear, or to put it another way, with Günther Anders:

"The relationship between man and the world becomes unilateral. The world, neither present nor absent, becomes a ghost."

The individual becomes artificial by constantly looking at screens, surfing the web endlessly, and even positioning themselves beyond the human. We are witnessing a disappearance of the sacred human person. The dreams of fanciful transhumanists endanger our already deeply wounded humanity. Do we need to be wounded further?

With smartphone life, man is not only scattered in the maze of abundant knowledge, he struggles to digest it, but also retains little from his multiple connections; his life unfolds like episodes that do not reach his consciousness because he lives with ghosts. Being overloaded with information, the smartphone user is hindered in digesting, reflecting, and thinking for himself. His mind is too guided by social networks, by screens: now smartphone connectionism has become his new religion. That is why he refuses to put away his smartphone.

[140]   Martin Buber: Je et tu, Aubier, 2012, Paris.

Gunther Anders: L'obsolescence de l'homme, Volume II, Éditions FARIO, 2011, p. 30, Paris.

Anders uses accurate words in the subtitle of his volume II of "L'obsolescence de l'homme, the notion of destruction of life in the era of the third industrial revolution". Indeed, with the misuse of digital technology, we are at the end of man, of his humanity, of what made him human (his thoughts, his freedom, his morality, his values of brotherhood, respect, concern for others...). Our techno-scientific, techno-medical, techno-digital postmodernity continues to want to modify man (his DNA), our being, to lead to the end of man thinking for himself. A new, very banal human born out of techno-scientific research will never be an authentic man. Man must not forget that he came out of the hands of nature and not from techno-scientific digital. With the foolish transhumanist project, we have fallen into nihilism, that is to say, into the loss of meaning, of values. Our smartphone life leads to the death of man, to the disappearance of the human and its limits. More precisely, we are in a radical nihilism illustrated by the fall of man, of his culture, of his millennia-old civilisation: all in total contradiction with man and his thoughts, replaced by the robot and the thought. By looking at smartphone screens, we no longer think for ourselves. We are drawing a propaedeutic to the transhuman or posthuman. It appears that posthumanism introduces a dangerous and discriminatory competition between the "classic" man, fruit of divine creation, and the new man-machine transhuman. It is in the double death of man and God that the postmoderns must think about our humanity questioned by the "advancements", the "progress" of techno-sciences.[135][136]

It follows that the idea of surpassing God was already present at the dawn of Promethean technology. For example, in his "Oration on the Dignity of Man" (1486), Pic de la Mirandole wants man to be a creator, master of his future. For him, thanks to technical progress, man will be able to "reach higher forms that are divine". Humanity has always aspired to a better life, and for that, it is ready to challenge God and to take on the role of God. Today, digital life is a reality, but we are going too far in the use of techno-sciences. The alternative is not between "putting away your phone" or "digesting your phone" (that is to say, understanding it, using it

141 G. Anders, Ibid., op. cit.
142 Ibid, op.cit.

with philosophy), but between the human and transhumanism: only the human in his relationship with others should matter because he is a being of feelings, emotions, true religion, and philosophy. Man must beware of the excessive use of digital gadgets, and his vocation is to encourage public discussion directly and not always through social networks, as these can be anti-social networks.[137][138]

Certainly, we must deal with the invasive techno-digital, but the lessons of past philosophers must have a good place. For example, Socrates was considered the wise man of Athens, Plato as the master of philosophy, and Aristotle as the professor of philosophy. They invite us to remain fully human and to think about man in his difficulties in eliminating contradictions through public discussion, to trust reason in a difficult human world. The notion of leaving the human condition is improper, even if it is sought today; that is to say, to move away from reason and the human in a smartphone and techno-scientific world. We are the children of nature, and we must cultivate the hope of remaining fully in it and using digital technology with discernment.[139]

The uncertainty of our world should worry us in order to control what techno-scientists are doing. Because all technology today is beyond the control of men, especially those who oppose any modification of our humanity: this is a very bad result of the death of man and the end of man. The smartphone is leading us towards the end of man thinking for himself. In the digital world, where is fraternity, peace, and harmony among men? Let us stop living "in a thought of precarious man or man amputated from man." We are at the end of man thinking for himself since he needs the digital. Man, human, humane, Man, are all attempts to express our humanity wounded by malevolent techno-science in the hands of certain scientific specialists, suspicious futurologists, dubious transhumanists, and posthumanists... These destroyers of humanity should be sent back to the "ubuntu" of the Bantu language. In fact, when we want to show the good we

---

143 With Günther Anders, we can establish the link between nihilism and the atomic bombIbid., p. 337.
144 Marin Pascal: Le robot et la pensée, Cerf, 2019, Paris.
[145]   G. Anders, op. cit.

think of someone, the Bantu says: "Yu, U UBUNTU", that is to say someone has UBUNTU: generosity, hospitality, friendship, humanity, compassion, and is ready to share what he has. This is a reminder that we must return to philosophical anthropology. The essence of ubuntu is this: "My humanity is intermingled, inextricably linked to yours."[140]

[150] Mungi Ngomane: Ubuntu, je suis car tu es. Leçons de sagesse africaine, édition Harper/ Collins, 2019, p. 22-2, Paris.

GENERAL BIBLIOGRAPHY

1. Anders Günther: - L'obsolescence de l'homme. Sur l'âme à l'époque de la deuxième révolution. industrielle (1956), éditions Ivrea, 2008, Paris - L'obsolescence de l'homme. Sur la destruction de la vie à l'époque de la troisième révolution industrielle, Tome II, édition Fario, 2011, Paris

2. ANDLER Daniel: Intelligence artificielle, intelligence humaine: la double énigme, Gallimard, 2023. Paris

3. ARENDT, Hannah: Condition de l'homme moderne, Calmann-Lévy, 2020, Paris. - La liberté d'être libre, Payot, 2019, Paris.

4. ARNOULT Jacques: Quand les hommes se prennent pour Dieu, Forum, 2020. Paris

5. ARISTOTE: Ethique à Nicomaque, Garnier Flammarion, 2004, Paris.

6. ATTALI, Jacques: Histoire des médias, Fayard, 2021, Paris.

7. BASTIE Eugénie: La guerre des idées, Robert Laffont, 2021, Paris.

8. BARTHES Roland: La chambre claire, Gallimard, 1980, Paris.

9. BENOIT XVI: Ce qu'est le christianisme, éditions du Rocher, 2023, Paris.

10. BESNIES Jean-Michel: Demain les posthumains, édition Pluriel, 2017. Paris.

11. BIRNBAUM, Jean (direction): Être humain? Gallimard, 2022. Paris.

12. BLOCQUAUX Stéphane: Le biberon numérique, Artège, 2021, Paris.

13. BLOOM, Allan: L'âme désarmée. Le déclin de la culture générale, Julliard, 1987, Paris.

14. BRAGUE Rémi: Le règne de l'homme, Gallimard, 2023, Paris.

15. BRIGHELLI Jean-Paul: La fabrique du crétin, éd. J.C. Gowsewitch, 2006, Paris.

16. BUBER Martin: Je et Tu, Aubier, 2012, Paris.

17. CANGUILHEM Georges: La connaissance de la vie, Vrin, 1967, Paris.

18. COLON David: Propagande. La manipulation de masse dans le monde contemporain, Flammarion, 2020, Paris

19. Comité national d'éthique numérique. Pour une éthique du numérique, P.U.F. 2021. Paris.

20. DELHEZ, Charles: Où allons-nous? De la modernité au transhumanisme, Salvator, 2018, Paris.

21. DEMURGET Michel: La fabrique du crétin digital. Les dangers des écrans pour nos enfants, Seuil, 2019, Paris.

22. DIESBACH de Louis: Liker sa servitude, FLY éditions, 2023, Paris.

23. DOUEIHI Milad, LOUZEAC Frédéric: Du matérialisme numérique, Herman, 2017, Paris.

24. DREHER Rod: Résister au mensonge. Vivre en chrétien dissident, Artège, 2021, Paris.

25. DROZ Geneviève: Les mythes platoniciens, Seuil, 1992, Paris.

26. EPICTETE: Manuel, Garnier-Flammarion, 1997, Paris.

27. FOUCAULT, Michel: Les mots et les choses, Gallimard, 1988, Paris.

28. GABRIEL Markus: Pourquoi la pensée humaine est inégalable? Edition J.C. Lattès, 2019. Paris

29. GERMAIN Éric (coordination): Pour une éthique du numérique, P.U.F., 2021. Paris

30. GIORGINI Pierre, MAGNIN Thierry: Vers une civilisation de l'algorithme? Un regard chrétien sur un défi éthique, Bayard, 2021, Paris.

31. GRINBAUM, Alexi: Paroles de machines, Humensciences, 1923, Paris.

32. HARARI Noah Yuval: Homo Deus: Une brève histoire du futur, Albin Michel, 2022. Paris

33. HEGEL: Leçons sur la philosophie de l'histoire, Vrin, 1987, Paris

34. HÉRACLITE (traduction de M. Conche): Fragments, P.U.F., 1986.

35. HOBBES, Thomas: Léviathan, éditions Dallez, 1998, Paris.

36. JEAN Amélie: De l'autre côté de la machine, édition de l'observatoire, 2019, Paris.

37. KAFKA, Franz: La métamorphose, Garnier-Flammarion, 2010, Paris.

38. KANT: Conjectures sur les débuts de l'histoire humaine, Le livre de Poche, 2018, Paris.

39. KOENIG Gaspard: La fin de l'individu. Voyage au pays de l'intelligence artificielle, Le point, 2019, Paris.

40. LA BOETIE (de) Étienne: Discours sur la servitude volontaire, Flammarion, 2016, Paris.

41. LACROIX Jean: «Le point de vue d'un philosophe,» article dans Morale sans péché? Cahier n°11 Recherches et Débats, Fayard, 1955, Paris

42. LANDI Giovanni: Intelligence artificielle comme philosophie, Les éditions Ovadio, 2022, Paris.

43. LEVINAS Emmanuel: Humanisme de l'autre homme, Le Livre de Poche, 1987, Paris.

44. MARIN Pascal: Le robot et la pensée, Cerf, 2019, Paris.

45. MONTAIGNE: Essais I, Le livre de Poche, 2015, Paris.

46. NIETZSCHE Frédéric: œuvre complète dans la collection Colli et Montinari, 14 volumes, 2002, Paris

47. NGOMANE Mungi: Ubuntu, je suis car tu es. Leçons de sagesse africaine, édition Harper, 2019, Paris, Paris

48. Pascal BLAISE, Pensées, Le livre de Poche, 1995.

49. PINAUDE, Florence; PERROTIN, Elodie: Qui sont les Transhumanistes? Édition du Ricochet, 2019, Paris.

50. PIECES ET MAIN D'OEUVRES: Manifeste des chimpanzés du futur, contre le transhumanisme, éditions Service compris, 2017, Paris

51. PUECH Michel: Homo sapiens technologicus, édition Le Pommier, 2016, Paris

52. PITRON Guillaume: L'enfer numérique. Voyage au bout d'un like, éditions Les Liens qui libèrent, 2021, Paris.

53. Platon: République, Garnier-Flammarion, 1984, Paris. - Protagoras, Garnier-Flammarion, 1997, Paris.

54. PRICE Catherine: Lâche ton téléphone, Librairie générale française, 2018, Paris.

55. Sadin Éric: L'ère de l'individu tyran, Grasset, 2020, Paris.

56. REDECKER, Robert: Réseaux sociaux: La guerre des Léviathans, Rocher, 2021, Paris.

57. RICOEUR Paul: Morale sans péché ou péché sans moralisme? Revue Esprit, 30-09-1954, Paris

58. SARAH Robert: Il a tant donné. Hommage à Benoit XVI, Fayard, 2023, Paris

59. TOCQUEVILLE, Alexis de: De la démocratie en Amérique, Garnier-Flammarion, 2010, Paris.

60. TOULOUSE, Anne: Wokisme, Rocher, 2022. Paris.

61. VANDERHEYDE Alphonse: «Nietzsche et la pensée bouddhiste», L'Harmattan, 2008, Paris. - La philosophie de la mort de l'homme. (Les acquis de la mort) de l'homme), 2008, éditions Connaissances et Savoirs, 2017, Paris - La fin de l'éducation de l'homme? (Tome 2: Les Acquis de La mort de l'homme, Connaissances et Savoirs, 2020, Paris.

62. VIDALIN Antoine: Personne! L'existence numérique ou la négation de la chair, Artège, 2021, Paris

63. ZUBOFF, Shoshana: L'âge du capitalisme de surveillance, édition Zulma, 2020, Paris.

64. ZWEIG Stephan: L'uniformisation du monde, édition Allia, 2021, Paris. Autres livres et revues.

- Le courrier international: le coup d'état numérique, hors-série, avril-mai 2021, Paris.

- La Bible de Jérusalem, notamment le livre de Ben Sira le sage.

- La Croix du 29-04-2023, Paris

- Philosophie magazine, Hors-série, IA, le mythe du XXe siècle, printemps 2023, Paris.

- Revue Études de septembre 2023, Paris: article de Philippe Forest: «La querelle du woke», p. 43-54.